THE 21st CENTURY AMERICAN

A NATIONAL CALL TO ACTION
TO SECURE THE BLESSINGS OF LIBERTY
TO OURSELVES AND OUR POSTERITY

{FROM AUTHOR}
ERIC COREY EPIFANO

The 21st Century American Patriot

This is a work of nonfiction. The author has written this work from his own knowledge and experience and takes full responsibility for the contents herein. Every effort has been made to give credit for any quotes and representations of others and historical figures. Nothing within this book is intended to demean any person living or dead. The opinions represented by the author are solely his own and not the representations of Big Thunder Publishing, its editors or staff.

Published by:
Big Thunder Publishing,

A wholly owned subsidiary of
Big Thunder, LLC
P.O. Box 82836,
San Diego, CA 92138

www.bigthunder.org

Cover Design by Christina Lutteroth

Interior Layout & Design by Scribe Freelance | www.scribefreelance.com

ISBN: 978-0-9821867-2-5
LC Control No.: 2009939906

Printed in the United States of America

Dedicated to my wife and my children.

Contents

Foreword

D*uring the unusually hot summer* of 1787, in the State House of Philadelphia, fifty-five delegates from twelve of the thirteen newly independent American colonies met to discuss the proposition of uniting these separate States to form a national government (only Rhode Island declined to send a delegation). The meetings were held in secret—not for some nefarious reason but to assure a focused civil debate and to eliminate undue outside influences. There was no official transcript to document the conversations and debates—we have only the extensive notes taken by James Madison, notes that were sometimes exact quotes and often paraphrased remembrances, to recall the proceedings.

The purpose of this assembly was to draft a Constitution that would serve as the law of these united lands and form a federal government that would fulfill the promise of the Declaration of Independence—assuring its citizens the guarantee of liberty and freedom through limited government. Begun on May 25th, 1787 and adjourned seventeen weeks later on September 17th, when thirty-nine delegates from twelve States signed the final draft of the Constitution and sent it on to the States for ratification, the Constitutional Convention is the gathering where the United States of America was originally conceived. The Constitution, with its preamble and Articles I through VII, was written at this Convention and continues to serve as the supreme law of the land to this day.

Prior to its ratification, furious debates raged as the publication of the proposed Constitution made its way though the colonies. Not everyone was in agreement with the proposal to form this union and very few had any understanding as to how it would operate. Coordinated efforts, both pro and con covered the States with articles, speeches and pamphlets to persuade the masses prior to the individual State's vote for ratification. Clear battle-lines were drawn between those in favor a federal government (Federalists) and those opposed to the idea (Anti-Federalists).

Alexander Hamilton, a delegate from New York, was the only one of the three delegates from that state who was *for* ratification. He recognized the absolute need for New Yorkers' approval in order to assure success in this effort and conceived a plan to bring about his desired outcome.

Hamilton decided on a writing campaign of unprecedented proportions to be published in all the New York newspapers that would describe the Constitution in specific terms and explain to the people of every State exactly how this new government would work. The writing effort would be carried out by three men, James Madison, Alexander Hamilton and John Jay, all writing under the pseudonym Publius. Together, they published a series of articles beginning in the fall of 1787 through the spring of 1788. Averaging nearly three articles per week, these men blanketed the New York print media with a constant barrage of information about the intentions and conclusions of the delegates at the Constitutional Convention that previous summer.

The eighty-five separate articles have become known as The Federalist Papers and provide the clearest understanding of Constitutional intent as described though a first hand account of the Convention's proceedings. The articles provide the supporting arguments for the need for a common defense, establishing a structure for commerce and trade amongst the States and enumerating the powers of the three, separate but equal branches of this form of government. Every aspect of the proposed Union is explained in great detail and supported by historical experience. Operating under the maxim that *"experience is the oracle of truth"*, Madison provides the basis on which the mechanics of the approved document were founded and often refers to the lessons of Greek and Roman attempts at democracy and their subsequent failings due to the limited ability of man to resist the natural temptations of corruption with power.

The Federalist Papers provide the written evidence of the framer's intent and act as the primary source for Constitutional interpretation. The first thirty-six articles deal with the need for a Union of States and the inadequacies of the Articles of Confederation—the standing agreement at that time among the thirteen States. The second section, articles thirty-seven through eighty-five, deal with the exact construction of the federal government and the duties, assignments and limitations of the legislative, executive and judicial branches.

The eloquent writing and deep subject matter make for timeless reading and provide a unique insight into the soul of our Founding Fathers. The 21st Century American Patriot relies on the spirit of our Constitutional Framers and attempts to apply their thinking in contemporary terms.

Chapter One

The Silver Bullet

"Governments are instituted among Men, deriving their just Powers from the Consent of the Governed, that whenever any Form of Government becomes destructive of the Ends, it is the right of the People to alter or to abolish it

—DECLARATION OF INDEPENDENCE

We *find ourselves at a crucial time* in our nation's history, much like our Founding Fathers, where we must act, not of desire but of desperation. Two hundred and thirty plus years after declaring independence from a tyrannical King, the people of these lands once again face a seemingly immovable force, one with great mass and entrenchment in control of our nation and leading its people down a path to certain and predictable financial destruction. There is nothing on the horizon that gives us any indication that this impending crisis will be addressed by those who control our fate. The time has come to call on the wisdom of our Founding Fathers and apply the mechanism made available by the creators of our Constitution and Bill of Rights to take decisive action and dissolve a legislative body in one election. I call it *The Silver Bullet.*

I *greatly debated with myself in deciding* the order of the presentation of the how and why of these proposed actions. Should I incite the reader with the recount of flagrant offensives and an impending financial collapse? Or should I first present a course of action that would illicit a high level of skepticism before a comprehensive argument can be made in its support? I have instead decided to start by endeavoring to reach down into every reader, to a level deep inside untouched by bias and selfish needs and rooted in common sense and decency—a place beyond the reach of nuanced arguments and irrelevant hyperbole. I'm hoping to find that place where the heart and mind merge to agree on a necessary course of action. You see, the proposition I present will ask you to take a leap of faith in humanity. To throw a national legislative body into disarray and hope for a greater outcome is to believe in the purity of ourselves and our ability to restore order.

The source of this power is clearly articulated in the debates of the Constitutional Conventions, Federalist Papers and the Constitution itself. If we believe in the genius of the framers of our national documents, then we must trust their insights into the nature of man and his propensity for corruption with power. It is clear, in a review of the constitutional debates and subsequent writings, that the founders foresaw a time of an entrenched national legislature and the need to provide a disenfranchised class of people, a mechanism to correct these regressions.

Nowhere is this concept more clearly articulated than in Alexander Hamilton's writings in the Federalist #61. While discussing the need for uniformity in election times for the Federal House of Representatives, Hamilton wrote;

> *"It is more than possible, that this uniformity may be found by experience to be of great importance to the public welfare; both as a security against the perpetuation of the same spirit in the body; and as a cure for the diseases of faction".*
>
> *"The consequence of this diversity* (addressing the proposal to stagger elections for the House of Representatives) *would be, that there could never happen a total dissolution or renovation of the body at one time. If an improper spirit of any kind should happen to prevail in it, that spirit would be apt to infuse itself into the new members as they come forward in succession. The mass would be likely to remain nearly the same; assimilating constantly to itself its gradual*

accretions. There is a contagion in example which few men have sufficient force of mind to resist. I am inclined to think that treble the duration in office, with the condition of a total dissolution of the body at the same time, might be less formidable to liberty, than one third of that duration, subject to gradual and successive alterations".

A total dissolution of the House of Representatives as a cure for the diseases of faction is the proposition that I put forth as the duty of a 21st Century American Patriot. It is a simple call to the citizens of our country to come together and commit to a most painless obligation to remove your representative from the House of Representatives, all in one election, for the greater good of our nation. I do not present this option with a frivolous mind, but with the support of our Founding Fathers. Could there be any doubt that if these men were alive today to see the condition of our nation's finances and equate that with a breed of career politicians that dominate legislative decisions that they would consider this anything but an *improper spirit* created by *the diseases of faction*?

These great men and women who gave their lives and risked everything to form these United States could never have imagined that the people of this country, in great numbers, would not take action to defend what they had created—that a complacent electorate would form and allow incompetent men and women with selfish motives to remain in charge of preserving the fruits of their sacrifice.

The simple task of casting a vote against any incumbent office holder in the House of Representatives does not require any special instructions or adherence to any specific political movement beyond that of preserving what our founders had created. Simply pull the lever (figuratively speaking) and let the Constitution take care of the rest.

This action does not lend itself to advocate a specific set of political principles or partisan ambitions. There is no political angle to be achieved and I am not a candidate for any office. This act, as endorsed by our Founding Fathers is an act of political necessity to reinstate the purpose of the House of Representatives—to bring men and women to this national post that will reintroduce the people's business and eliminate a class of perpetual politicians.

It is clear in a review of the debates at the Constitutional Convention of 1787 that the founders had envisioned a branch of the national legislative body that would come directly from the people. In discussions regarding the formation of what would become known as the House of Representatives, Eldridge Gerry the delegate from Massachusetts argued that;

> *"the government ought to possess not only first the force, but secondly the mind or sense of the people at large. The Legislature ought to be the most exact transcript of the whole Society"*

George Mason of Virginia stated,

> *"The requisites on actual representation are that the Representatives should sympathize with their constituents; should think as they think, and feel as they feel; and that for these purposes should even be residents among them".*

And (as noted by James Madison) James Wilson of Pennsylvania

> *"contended strenuously for drawing the most numerous branch of the Legislature immediately from the people".*

Not only did the creators of our Constitution not fear a legislature made up of common citizens without political experience, they clearly saw this as necessary in the proper execution of government and felt it mandatory to establish balance between the government and its people.

James Madison wrote extensively to this point in Federalist #63,

> *"in doubtful cases, particularly where the national councils may be warped by some strong passion, or momentary interest, the presumed or known opinion of the impartial world, may be the best guide that can be followed.... It is evident that the Senate must first be corrupted, before it can attempt an establishment of tyranny. Without corrupting the state legislatures, it cannot prosecute the attempt, because the periodical change of members would otherwise regenerate the whole body. Without exerting the means of corruption with equal success on the house of representatives, the opposition to that co-equal branch of the government would inevitably defeat the attempt; and without corrupting the people themselves, a succession of new representatives would speedily restore all things to their pristine order."*

It is precisely because there is not a sufficient regeneration of new members that this branch of government has lost that balance required to function as designed. Madison refers to this as an *"irresistible force... of a free government, which has the people on its side."* Those who hold these positions as permanent have become politically and financially infused with the Senate and do not serve the people as intended. They cannot be made to recognize the contradiction they create while serving in the house of the people, but they can be removed.

The intellect that produced The Constitution of the United States and the unequaled prosperity resulting from its execution has not let us down in the two plus centuries since its inception. I ask that you entrust this brilliance with our future and employ the technique provided in our founding to restore order and create a setting to resolve our nation's ills.

The final paragraph of Federalist #63 provides an eerily accurate prediction and an equally clear solution,

> *"Besides the conclusive evidence resulting from this assemblage of facts, that the federal senate will never be able to transform itself, by gradual usurpations, into an independent and aristocratic body; we are warranted in believing that if such a revolution should ever happen from causes which the foresight of man cannot guard against, the house of representatives with the people on their side will at all times be able to bring back the constitution to its primitive form and principles. Against the force of the immediate representation of the people, nothing will be able to maintain even the constitutional authority of the senate, but such a display of enlightened policy, and an attachment to the public good, as will divide with that branch of the legislature, the affections and support of the entire body of the people themselves".*

This ability to understand the precise nature of the corruptible effects of power and call on the lessons of history to predict future events this accurately, compels us to entrust these insights and obligates us to follow the procedure of total dissolution, as prescribed, if we hope to bring about tangible change and correct the transgressions of the unscrupulous.

And while this action would be of great significance, it does not represent the most important aspect of the undertaking. The silver in the silver bullet is reserved for the awakening of an electorate. The massive sector of the voting age population that consists of the disheartened and detached voter, those who have given up, convinced that the entire system is corrupt beyond repair—constitutes a super-majority, yet unaware of their collective strength and influence. Once this segment of the population is revived through this unified action and successfully dictates a new national direction, the realization of our might will revitalize an otherwise complacent electorate. Having at once executed our collective mind set will transform a generation of apathetic voters into engaged and rejuvenated protectors of liberty.

If this action is successful, every elected official in this country will recognize the coalescence of the masses, working in unity, exercising its constitutional power to create a new class of representation, one elected by the people, for the people and now, directly accountable to the people. Just imagine the impact you can have on the business as usual in Washington D.C. simply by choosing to not vote for the incumbent. Lobbyists with special access to the legislative agenda, drawn from years of monetary patronage to reelection coffers will find themselves without a champion. Career politicians will suddenly find that their perceived power and prestige is no longer protected by an unlimited flow of campaign cash. Fresh faced Congressional Representatives entering office with the understanding that their new powers are derived directly from the consent of the governed and that the condition of their reelection will be fixed to the unmistakable requirement to correct decades of incompetence borne of special interest pandering. Most importantly, a previously disengaged electorate will find itself firmly in control of their nation's destiny.

This revolution will be felt in every quarter of the nation. Media outlets of all political persuasions will not be able to ignore or spin the consequence of these actions. This simple act, to remove all incumbents in the House of Representatives in one election, will transform the national agenda and force the focus on the will of the people and cancel the effects of money in legislative decisions. If our Constitution came with operating instructions, this would be the Ctrl+ Alt+Delete protocol.

Many will have a difficult time voting against their local representative because of preexisting relationships and local successes. Your representative just might be the one guy who is trying to make a difference. If making a difference is what you're looking for, you can have no greater impact than to execute this plan. You must evolve beyond the ties that bind you to local importance and reach for higher recognition. Any slug can play it safe and figure "it's better the devil you know". While it will take great courage for many people to remove a local icon from office, you can take some solace in knowing that their retirement package is second to none. Know that it will be for a greater cause, one founded in constitutional principles and based on sound judgment.

If partisan politics is important to you and reconfiguring the Congressional majorities is an aspect in this venture you cannot accept, then it will be important for you to get involved in the primaries to nominate a candidate for the general election consistent with your party affiliation. To be clear, I am not advocating electing incompetent gadflys with narrow agendas, we are talking about your neighbor or local merchant, a friend or family member, anyone that lives in your district with political aspirations and a patriotic fire. As a responsible citizen of this country you must find it important to develop an informed opinion of these candidates. There will be qualified people from both major parties running in your local primaries that will provide you a sense of confidence in their ability to execute the office. Better yet, run for office yourself, it's surprisingly easy to become a candidate for the United States House of Representatives.

It won't matter which of the major political parities gains or loses seats or majority rule. What will absolutely matter is that the people of this country will have come together to state in clear and unequivocal terms that they are taking back this house of the people and that whom-so-ever shall make up this branch of government must attend to the people's business and be less concerned with party loyalty and more concerned with loyalty to country. Third party candidates may also make in-roads to the halls of power, but their assignment will be no more or no less accountable to the will of the citizenry. Party politics, in this instance, will only serve to provide some sense of direction to the electorate but will cease to be the determining factor in electoral outcomes.

Our Founding Fathers had great insight into the nature of man. They had foreseen this inevitability and they have seen to it that the people be given the power to correct a disastrous situation and misrepresentation of their will. I simply ask that you use the tools provided by these great men to return discipline, decency and accountability to the House of Representatives by voting to remove every incumbent from this office in one election.

Chapter Two

The Directive

There are so many reasons why a complete dissolution of the House of Representatives is necessary at this time in our nation's history—it is difficult to know where to begin. Clearly, there is no greater question that must be answered than how to restore financial responsibility, order and solvency to our nations finances. We are heading down a path to certain financial ruin without significant correction. Social issues and policy are not part of this discussion because without restoring fiscal discipline, we will not have the luxury of debate. Clouding this action with a specific political agenda, other than that of a return to fiscal responsibility, will greatly reduce its ability to succeed. We cannot allow the potential unity of this newly formed electorate to be threatened by partisanship. If we find success, we can find strength and relevance. Every other year we will exercise our unified power until people are elected who will answer the question and do what is necessary to solve the problem. We simply ask for a Congress who will provide a financial statement with accurate projections of future revenues, balance expenditures, reduce the size and scope of government and establish a plan to retire our nations' debt.

Most of you will not need convincing that this is the overriding issue that directly threatens our way of life and the single most important reason for this action. We must rally around the facts—facts that are extremely difficult to comprehend and equally difficult to face. If you are remotely paying attention, you know that the federal government spends significantly more than it receives in revenues. Future financial obligations are absolutely unsustainable based on any projection. The mathematic models have been built and run, the verdict is in – our nation is going broke at a breakneck pace and there is no plan to address, let alone resolve the issue.

Since 1992 The United States Government Accountability Office, (GAO) has provided Congress with long term financial simulations of "what might happen to federal deficits and debt levels under varying policy assumptions". At the request of Congress, the GAO has developed models to chart the long term effects of the current financial policies of Congress. Here's what they have been telling the incumbents as far back as 1993;

> BUDGET POLICY Long-Term Implications of the Deficit;
> Testimony before the Senate Finance Committee 3/25/1993
> *If we were to continue our recent spending and tax policies, our projections show deficits exploding to 20 percent of gross national product (GNP) by 2020… We do not believe this scenario can occur because we would face financial crisis before we reached that point, but the trends that produce the result are instructive. The steep increase in the projected deficit after 2010 reflects the symbiotic relationship of the growing debt and the increased interest costs associated with financing it, as well as rising retirement and health care costs. In our model this is happening in the environment of an economy whose growth is slowed by the debilitating effect of the deficits on national savings and investment. Indeed, in the final years of the projection period, the model shows the economy actually contracting.*

> BUDGET ISSUES Deficit Reduction and the Long Term;
> Testimony before the House Budget Committee 3/13/1996
> *The increased spending is principally a function of escalating federal spending on health care and Social Security, which is driven by projected rising health care costs and the aging of our population. Spending on interest on our national debt also rises as annual deficits*

and accumulated public debt expand. Essentially, current commitments in these areas become progressively unaffordable for the nation over time. Without any significant changes in spending or revenues, such an expanding deficit would result in collapsing investment, declining capital stock, and, inevitably, a declining economy by 2025.

LONG-TERM CARE Aging Baby Boom Generation Will Increase Demand and Burden on Federal and State Budgets; Testimony before Senate Special Committee on Aging 3/21/2002

To move into the future with no changes in federal health and retirement programs is to envision a very different role for the federal government. Our long-term budget simulations serve to illustrate the increasing constraints on federal budgetary flexibility that will be driven by entitlement spending growth. Assume, for example, that last year's tax reductions are made permanent; revenue remains constant thereafter as a share of GDP, and discretionary spending keeps pace with the economy. Under these conditions, spending for net interest, Social Security, Medicare, and Medicaid would consume nearly three-quarters of federal revenue by 2030. This will leave little room for other federal priorities, including defense and education. By 2050, total federal revenue would be insufficient to fund entitlement spending and interest payments.

LONG-TERM FISCAL CHALLENGE Comments on the Bipartisan Task Force for Responsible Fiscal Action Act; 10/31/2007

The bottom line is that the nation's longer-term fiscal outlook is daunting under any realistic policy scenario or assumptions. Continuing on this unsustainable fiscal path will gradually erode, if not suddenly damage, our economy, our standard of living, and ultimately our national security. Our current path also increasingly will constrain our ability to address emerging and unexpected budgetary needs and increase the burdens that will be faced by future generations.

The Nations Long Term Financial Outlook, September 2008 Update; 11/06/2008

Recently the President, the Congress, and the American people have been focused on addressing problems with financial markets and the appropriate response to a weakening economy. However, once the current challenges are resolved, the next President, the next Congress, and the nation will need to focus with the same intensity on the nation's long-term fiscal challenge... Our updated simulations continue to show escalating and persistent deficits that illustrate the long term fiscal outlook is unsustainable. The federal government faces large and growing structural deficits driven primarily by rising health care costs and known demographic trends. Furthermore, these simulations do not yet reflect recent actions taken by the federal government to support the financial sector.

This is but a small sampling of the warnings and projections provided Congress (at their request) by the GAO of an impending financial calamity. Still nothing has changed—to the contrary, the current 111th Congress, convened in 2009 has plans to accelerate deficit spending three fold and grow the national debt to levels beyond comprehension. All this in the face of a crumbling economy, near record unemployment and a looming Social Security and Medicare cost explosion. And still, there are no plans to even address the issue of ever increasing entitlement expenditures.

In lieu of providing pie charts and confusing graphs of federal revenues and spending, I have put together a view of the spending habits of current and futures Congress' that will be exceedingly easy to understand. Using numbers provided by the Congressional Budget Office[1] and by dropping a few zeros, I can clearly explain federal spending in more personal terms.

Let's say that in 2009 you personally will earn $21,590, but you will spend $40,040. To make up the difference you will borrow $18,450 just to meet the financial obligations that you have set for yourself. Since you have been doing this for 35 of the last 39 years[2] (spending more than you earn) your total debt at the end of 2008 was $58,027. After 2009 your new total debt owed will be $76,477. In 2010 you're projecting that you will earn $22,890 but once again you plan to spend $36,690 and will borrow another $13,790 to accommodate your spending habits. Now, at the end of 2010 you will be $90,267 in debt. Since you are paying only the interest on your debt, your principle has grown each and every year and you have no plan to pay down any of that principle. On the contrary, you have committed to obligations that will grow your debt as far into the future as you care to consider.

Now, add eight zeros to all of these numbers and you will see exactly what Congress has planned for our nation's financial future.

Any reasonable person would look at your financial management skills and conclude you're an idiot. No one would take pity on your desperate situation or try to deflect blame for your reckless spending habits. Certainly no one in their right mind would allow you to manage money under any circumstances and if it was your job to properly manage a company's finances you would have been fired years ago.

You see, it doesn't matter who is in control of Congress, or who sits in the office of the President, these reckless spending habits have been a

---

[1] "Comparison of Projected Revenues, Outlays and Deficits in CBO's March 2009 Baseline and CBO's Estimate of the Presidents Budget" Congressional Budget Office 20 March 2009.
[2] Table F1 "Revenues, Outlays, Surpluses, Deficits and Debt Held by Public-1969-2008" Congressional Budget Office 13 January 2009

constant for decades. And because there is no threat from a compliant electorate, those in charge of our nation's purse strings have no motivation to rectify the situation.

Unless there is a significant change in the configuration of Congress, this situation will continue and no corrections will be made as evidenced by the refusal of any member of Congress to deal with the matter. If you take the $1.845 trillion projected deficit for the 2009 federal budget and divide that number by 365, you will find that in 2009 our federal government plans to *borrow* over $5 billion dollars *each and every day* just to meet its obligations. Beyond that, under current policy, the United States Treasury has plans to continue borrowing against future revenues, approximately $900 billion dollars per year in each of the next 9 years beyond 2010. There is absolutely no end in sight and no plan to resolve this dramatic imbalance. If these were your personal finances, how long could you survive financially? How long before your bank stops lending you this money? How will you ever begin to pay any of this back? And what happens when they call in the debt?

Well, this is your personal finances, because the government does not generate any revenues beyond what it takes from its citizens. We the people of this country are the debtors and those who have put us in this position will be dead or well fed in retirement when this house of cards collapses on us, our children and their children.

It is beyond debate that this rising tide of debt is the single greatest threat to our nation's future economy and security. We do not have the money to continue to operate in this manner and we cannot sustain this course of deficit spending. Those in charge of our nation's finances are not oblivious to these facts—they rely on our ignorance and provide only lip service to our concerns.

Ask your incumbent Congressional Representative how he or she plans to address this dire situation. There is no plan except for this one—dissolve the entire House of Representatives every two years until we have seated a legislative body who will properly address the matter. This is the only act that will give legislators the required motivation to do the heavy lifting necessary to bring about real change to our financial future. It shouldn't take more than two or three election cycles to bring about the needed changes and put in place those who will follow more sound financial principles.

Because there is no motivation to curb spending, members of Congress do not feel threatened by the mounting debt. Each member of the House of Representatives has a fabulous retirement program that will continue to pay them 80%[3] of their final year's salary until death (even then their spouse will continue to receive benefits until their death). And after years of pandering to Capital Hill lobbyists who out number members of Congress 28 TO 1 [4], the chances of landing a lucrative job after retirement are all but guaranteed. As long as they spend tax payer dollars to keep the special interest concerns happy, they can count on an endless flow of campaign contributions for reelection. Combined with the franking privileges (free postage) and earmark spending (federal funds for pet projects in their home districts) reelection is a mere formality in the quest for personal aggrandizement.

Nothing will change this pattern of decadence and ignorance except a revolution at the ballot. We can elect a new President from a different party every four years, but the spirit in Congress that has remained intact for decades will remain consistent in their contempt for the people at large. The only way to break this cycle of deceit is to remind these public servants that they derive their power for the consent of the governed. Until which time the governed revoke their consent, nothing in Congress will change.

---

[3] "Retirement Benefits for Member of Congress" Report for Congress Congressional Research Service 8 February 2009.
[4] Lobbying Data Base; Center for Responsive Politics

http://www.opensecrets.org/lobby/index.php 20 March 2009

We must seat a revitalized House of Representatives, regardless of its political makeup, who will clearly understand the circumstance of their appointment, knowing that their election comes with a condition of quick removal in 24 months if they do not adequately address their fiscal responsibilities. This branch of government will no longer be accountable to political action committees or party hierarchy—this branch will be answerable to the electorate, as designed.

The day to day operations of this new Congress will be run by staff that has traditionally managed the affairs of each member. There will be no learning curve and no great catastrophe will befall our nation because inexperienced legislators will replace the career politician. This will be the argument put forth by the incumbent to dissuade you from utilizing this means to correct their ineptitude. They have no viable argument in this regard. The proof of their bungling is a matter of official record from which they cannot escape. They will blame the problems facing our country of members of the opposite party with contorted arguments designed to confuse and play on your perceived ignorance of the duties of Congress.

As the constitution clearly defines the roles of these legislatures in plain language, you will be armed with the facts that cannot be spun to justify years of compliance to special interest agendas and ineffectual representation. Do not be fooled by those who tell you that they are doing what is in the best interest of the country—no member of Congress cares about the country more than the continuation of their high position and office. If this were the case, they would have acted long ago to correct the obvious destruction of future prosperity instead of voting in the lockstep of party unity and frivolously spending taxpayer dollars to secure reelection.

This cannot be understated—it is the nature of man to defend his territory, especially when that turf comes with the power and prestige of elected office. The temptation of this dangerous preeminence will warp the will and integrity of even the strongest among us. This rejuvenation of Congress cannot physically occur without the involvement of the citizenry working in concert to prevent this inherent allure of corruption. It is our mission and constitutional duty as the governed, to keep the members of the House of Representatives anchored and in check by recycling their ranks in order to maintain the proper mindset required to fulfill the role of this legislative body as intended.

Chapter Three

My Congressman

When I was young and naive and filled with a patriotic fire, I had an irresistible urge to serve my country. I understood one thing – our nation's most pressing problems could most effectively be addressed through the acts of Congress. I believe that the power to write legislation to attend to the financial malaise our nation faces can be accomplished most directly through this body. With nothing more than some community service behind me, I entered the primary in my congressional district by collecting signatures for my nomination and filing the proper paperwork. I was a candidate for the United States House of Representatives in 1990 in California's 44th Congressional District and 1992, in the newly formed 52nd Congressional District. My experiences as a candidate in these two Congressional primaries provided a window into the soul of the people who succeed and proposer in this field. What I have concluded, in my subsequent experiences, is that what these people (career politicians) generally lacked was the same thing I was taught to honor most—personal integrity. Not that I haven't done things in my life that I am ashamed of, because I have—it's just that I considered this high position of public trust required, above all, honesty and integrity in the service of our nation.

I grew up less than 5 miles from Independence Mall in Philadelphia and vigorously studied the founding of our nation. I felt a close bond to that place and to those who toiled there to form these United States. I saw myself as one of these men—a person dedicated to the promise of our Constitution and a defender of its propositions of life, liberty and the pursuit of happiness. I was prepared to live my life as a staunch supporter of these principles and to carry on the work of these great men.

I eventually concluded that I could never be successful in any election because I was unwilling to compromise my personal beliefs and undermine my personal integrity in the quest to secure votes. In tight primary races every group of voters was important. As a candidate you could not go to a speaking engagement or debate without tailoring your positions to pander to the host sponsors if you had any hope of securing their votes. Often, I would have to hold my tongue and not speak my position honestly—compromising what I believed for the purpose of getting support from a room full of guaranteed voters. This I could not do. The successful political candidate who was skilled in this endeavor spoke very carefully so as to not offend any potential voter, usually saying nothing at all (a very unique skill). To be fair, had I been successful, I cannot say how the taste of power may have eventually distorted my better judgment. I can only speak to the life I have lead as a devoted husband and father and compared it to that of those who defeated me in these two primaries and went on to win in the general election. One is currently in jail for accepting money and gifts in exchange for government contracts in the most celebrated Congressional corruption scandal in U.S. history. The other has distinguished himself as one of the many representatives who, until caught, provided himself with 399 interest free loans through the now closed House Bank, and cashed campaign checks, until caught, at the now closed House Post Office. The latter also managed to secure his 15 term House seat for his son, to continue in his entrenched footsteps. In that time I have—along with my wife, raised three children and founded a successful business, all based on a foundation of honesty and integrity.

I do not speak of these men with ill will or any desire to degrade them personally or hold myself up as their better. I simply wish to provide these two particular men as an example of the successful politician, as I have experienced them. This is to not paint every member of Congress as criminal or dishonest, it is only to illustrate the nature of this beast and to help you understand that ultimately, this is something of our own creation.

Each and every time we vote for the incumbent in the House of Representatives, we condone the behavior of this legislative body as a whole. No one person can vote in any Congressional district but their own, leaving each of us only one vote to approve or reject the actions of this branch of our national legislature. Since we have not acted—unified with a common goal of accurate representation, we have allowed the influences of special interest concerns to direct the actions of our representatives. We give incumbent politicians no reason to address the concerns of the majority because the majority does not participate in the process. Make no mistake, unless you vote to remove your Congressional representative from the House of Representatives, they will have no incentive to change their pattern of behavior. We have allowed the unlimited flow of politically positioned money determine the outcome of elections and dictate policy decisions because we do not act to change it. If you are looking for the culpable, you need look no further than the closest mirror.

It is time we see ourselves as the ones who control government instead of accepting the flawed idea that government controls us. As American citizens we can arm ourselves with a constitutionally established provision to dissolve the House of Representatives in one election, to take back control of this nation and return the critical decision making to its people. People who have spent their lives raising children, balancing checkbooks, creating neighborhoods, working for the weekend and respecting their country and fellow man. These are the people who we can entrust with the future of our nation. These are the people who will do what is in the best interest of our country without the constraints of prepaid obligations to Washington's elite.

The House of Representatives was not created for the men and women who now populate it chambers, it was created for the common man who must provide balance to a Senate with larger political propensities and moorings. We have done our Founding Fathers a deep injustice by allowing this legislative body to act with aristocratic immunity. Their inability to correct the glaring improprieties with regard to our nation's finances has shown them to be more concerned with reelection than the need to address their own incompetence. To effectively do so will require them to forfeit their perceived power and bite the hand from which they feed.

The House of Representatives is no place for the career politician—it is the house of the people. By returning the House of Representatives to the people, we can begin the process of setting things right. Not that I know exactly what setting things right entails, I only know that people, unencumbered by the need for perpetual political position will have a much better chance of setting things right than those with personal political agendas and grand aspirations of relevance.

Your Congressman follows the same pattern of conduct as mine—always jockeying to get the key committee assignment or prestigious office space. Working with party loyalists to secure financial contributions and stuffing campaign coffers with enough cash to discourage opposition and perpetuate permanency. All this requires an adherence to the business as usual standard of lining one's pockets and those of your best friends and political supporters. If you doubt that your representative is of this ilk, I challenge you to partake in a simple exercise that will prove otherwise.

The Federal Election Commission requires that all political contributions to candidates for public office be reported. These reports are readily available to the public and can easily be accessed through the FEC's web site. Every elected official must report the amount received and the name of the donor. It is easy to track the source of money and just as easy to track the voting records and committee testimony of your elected representative. By simply overlaying these two records, you will be able to understand the correlation between members voting habits and the agendas of their campaign contributors.

Following your Representatives voting record is effortless since most local newspapers regularly publish these votes—it's the committee testimony that is slightly more difficult and extremely tedious to follow. There is however, a much simpler way to prove this pay for play standard, its called earmarks.

Earmarks are discretionary spending that allows each member to direct federal funds to home districts and pet causes. There is nearly unanimous bi-partisan support for this contentious spending scheme that allows members of Congress to loot the Federal Treasury (at their discretion) and reward those who financially supported their candidacy to assure their place at a bountiful table filled with your wage withholdings. Tracking these earmark spending requests has just recently become much easier to follow since the 111th Congress is now requiring members to report earmark requests on their web sites.

My Congressman is Duncan Hunter—he was first elected to the House of Representatives in 1981 and has been there ever since. When I reviewed Representative Hunter's FEC report[5] it showed that in the 2005/2006 election cycle alone, he collected $1,063,228 in campaign contributions (an extraordinary number when you consider that the job only pays $157,000 per year). The list of individual and corporate (political action committee) contributors in this report was page upon page of a who's who in America. You name the corporation or labor union, and their political action committee gave money to my representative. Without regard to political affiliation, political action committees contribute to all incumbents to cover their bets and assure

---

[5] "Candidate (HsCA42023 Summary Reports – 2005-2006 Cycle, Federal Election Commission 31 Dec 2006

access to the next Congress. My Congressman's list is staggering, filled with corporate names everyone will recognize; AT&T, Blue Shield, Boeing, Bechtel, Chevron, Cummins, Continental Airlines, General Electric, General Dynamics, General Atomic, Goodrich, Goodyear, Lockheed Martin, Halliburton, Honeywell, Johnson Controls, Lucent Technologies, Qualcom, Rolls Royce, UPS, Federal Express, Walgreen's, Texas Instruments, Weyerhaeuser, Caterpillar, Raytheon, Cubic Corporation, the list goes on and on. He received money from beet growers, avocado growers and sugar beet farmers. From labor association's political action committees for airline pilots, firefighters, boilermakers and various other employee service unions, far too numerous to list here.

The National Associations of Uniformed Services, Chain Drug Stores, Realtors, Insurance and Financial Advisors all gave him money. Beer wholesalers, nurse anesthetists, orthodontists, chiropractors, dental associations also donated to his campaign. This is but a small sampling of the entire list and does not include the hundreds of individual contributors, many of whom work in the industries and for the same corporations named above.

Since my Congressman, in 2008, was not required to post his earmark spending requests on his web site, obtaining this information was a bit more difficult, but not much. Taxpayers for Common Sense an *"independent and non-partisan voice for taxpayers working to increase transparency and expose and eliminate corrupt subsidies, earmarks, and corporate welfare"* provided the necessary information.

Congressman Hunter requested a total of $28.2 million for his earmark spending needs in 2008. The bulk of this money, $15.2 million went to L-3 Communications, Advanced Systems Division for *"affordable weapons systems"*. Another $1.2 million went to Trex Enterprises Corporation for *"cable warning & obstacle avoidance systems"*. He also requested $1 million to Chenoweth Racing Products for *"light vehicles*". The observable and undeniable quid pro quo is laid bare when you compare this list with the list of donors from his FEC report referenced above.

L-3 Communications Corporation Political Action Committee donated $15,000 to Duncan Hunter's campaign in 2005. The President and Vice President of this corporation also donated a combined $4,350 as individual contributors. It is hard to escape the fact that the $15.2 million federal check this company received represents a 78,450% return on their money—money that was wisely invested with my Congressional Representative. Trex Enterprise Corporation donated, through individual contributions from their CEO, CFO, President, Vice President and Engineer totaling $3,125—a 38,300% return on their money. And Chenoweth Racing Products President donated a paltry $250 for the $1 million in taxpayer money he received (+ $999,750).

When Duncan Hunter relinquished his seat to make a run at the Presidency in 2008, he bequeathed his political capitol to his son, Duncan D. Hunter who inherited his father's organization and political machinery that he built over a 27 year career. The replacement Hunter won in a landslide mainly due to name recognition that rendered his $1.3 million in campaign contributions unnecessary. Duncan D., the ever compliant son, continued his father's work of directing federal funds to campaign contributors through the earmark process.

According to the junior Hunter's Federal Election Commission report[6], he received $7,300 from General Atomics Political Action Committee and another $9,000 from the CEO, President and Vice Chair of General Dynamics Corporate entity. This garnered them a $26 million dollar earmark request from Representative Hunter for the fiscal year 2010 budget, according to his web site. Trex Enterprises

[6] "Candidate (H2CA42023) Summary Reports – 2007-2008 Cycle" Federal Election Commission 31 Dec 2008

Corporation also received another $3 million earmark, or as Duncan D. puts it, *"funding initiative"* in the 2010 budget. It is no coincidence that Trex Enterprises Corporation's CEO, President, Vice Chair, Manager, Engineer, Scientist, Sales Rep and Lawyer contributed another $6,000 combined, to fund his campaign.

This is just an infinitesimal scratching of the surface in the illustration of how money determines spending priorities and government policy in the House of Representatives. Because these members of Congress have contributor lists that are so vast and all-encompassing, there is rarely a vote cast by a member of Congress that does not affect the enterprise of someone on that list. I am not so naive as to recognize that this political chicanery is common practice at all levels of government and I am certainly not surprised by my findings.

Now what? Are we to roll our eyes and say, oh well… that's just the way it is and accept this manipulation of a system originally created to prevent this exact abuse of the public trust? The old guard will surely defend this paradigm as the way business has been and will always be done in Washington and arrogantly dismiss these accusations as unenlightened opposition.

This is precisely the glitch in the system and error in the machinery of government that our founders had foreseen. This exploitation of our system of governance feeds into the weakness of man and creates the corruption that infuses itself upon its members to establish a brotherhood of common criminals with the power to perpetrate their dastardly deeds with condescending immunity.

The obligation to these interests inferred when money changes hands is undeniable and inescapable for the recipient. These groups acquire special access to legislators through the exchange of money and demand adherence to their specific political causes. The vast majority of a representative's constituency does not enjoy similar access because they do not have as great an affect on the representative's political future as do these powerful political action committees, organized labor groups and corporate entities. Reversing this pattern will require a greater participation and coordinated effort of an electorate who must take a more aggressive role in these proceedings and object to this accepted practice by simply withholding their vote.

Your representative will profess his or her allegiance to their constituents, and certainly they must to secure your votes, but their true obligations are to the lobbyists who walk the halls of Capitol Hill carrying with them the political power of persuasion through the financial support they provide. To deny this quid pro quo exists is offensive to even the most naive among us. You may not find this as offensive for a member of the U.S. Senate since they have a broader political sphere of influence and represent larger concerns—but for a member of the House of Representatives, this conduct is contrary to the Constitutional mandate of their office.

Only when these well funded political concerns are marginalized, can the representative carry out the true representation envisioned by the founders. If this effort is successful, the newly elected representative will understand that reelection will only be secured by carrying out the will of the people and not by pandering to those who will provide funding for reelection campaigns.

You may think you have representation in Washington D.C., but you do not. You have only a politician telling you what you want to hear while they are in town and doing what they need to do when they are not. The D.C. beltway is a strange and intoxicating place for the men and women who carry with them the power and ability to steer government spending and tailor federal regulations in favor of those who's job it is to secure your taxpayer dollars. The power of persuasion and promise of perpetual prominence that Washington lobbyists provide your representative does not stand a chance against your local concerns and single vote. Only a unified effort, as described herein, will change the course of our nation's history and restore the promise of our representative republic.

Chapter Four

SYSTEM MALFUNCTION

There is some irony to be had here—that the very thing I'm attempting to make happen (removal of incumbents in the House of Representatives) occurred in my very district in the 2008 election. In this case however, the newly elected member, or more accurately described replacement, had his place reserved for him by the previous incumbent—his father. As a King might pass the mantle of the throne to the next in line to continue the family birth-right, my representative had no resistance what-so-ever in securing this district for his son. This serves as a glaring example of how an audacious class of people acts to maintain dominance over their compliant subjects.

The seating of any new member of Congress cannot be left to chance—those in places of high authority who determine these things are firmly in control of this seat and all the influence and power it wields. And since my district traditionally votes in huge majorities for one of the major parties, the leaders of this party control the destiny of this seat. The 435 seats available in the House of Representatives are very important to these very important people. It is the primary job of party leadership to thoroughly determine their party's chances in each and every Congressional district across America and aggressively pursue, then support a candidate within the party structure, in that district, who will do their bidding and maintain the business as usual standard.

There is no place here for the common man or ideologue, only party loyalists who will play by the rules, tow the party line and not make waves. Once the party selects the candidate to fill a vacancy or run in a district where the incumbent is vulnerable for various reasons, the party machine is turned on to provide the unlimited funding necessary to discourage opposition outside this clique and assure the continuation of this ruling class.

And so maintains the established tyranny that James Madison assured us could not exist under this form of government known as a representative republic. An indoctrination of thought and compliance with party policy completely fuses the new member to the body of Congress, acting in unison and in preservation of each other. The system established maintains and sustains those who have made careers and fortunes feeding from the teat of government. The United States Congress will spend nearly $3 trillion in 2009—with such large sums of money in play, these professionals and well placed concerns swim like whales in the warm waters of limitless funding, feeding on the plankton of the masses. Separating these big fish from their food source cannot be accomplished by those on the inside who are charged with keeping these creatures nourished. This heavy lifting can only be achieved by the detached and uncorrupted—people who can accurately represent the hundreds of millions of Americans on the outside struggling for their piece of this American pie. These are the people without a champion in government and represent the missing element in the equation of a successfully operational bi-cameral legislature. Only people without a bias borne of paid servitude to established governmental interests are properly equipped to fulfill the requirements of this office. Only people outside this sphere of influence and mindset can stabilize a ship so fundamentally listing under the weight of its own self indulgence.

This loss in balance between the House of Representatives and the U.S. Senate is the fundamental failing of the current Congressional system, with its companion electoral domination that has lead to run-away government and the gross misrepresentation of its citizenry. Once again, the founders saw this coming as James Madison wrote:

> *"The people can never willfully betray their own interests: But they may possibly be betrayed by the representatives of the people; and the danger will be evidently greater where the whole legislative trust is lodged in the hands of one body of men, than where the concurrence of separate and dissimilar bodies is required in every public act".* Federalist #63

The House and Senate have so completely fused into "*one body of men*" that the system has ceased to function as designed, creating such a detachment from the will of the people as to render it incapable of fulfilling its mission as a house of the people. As constructed, the bi-cameral legislature has a Senate that provides the stable institution required for the learned execution of legislative government and where greater ambition and corruption were predicted. A true house of the people is the critical check and balance mechanism incorporated into this legislative body, purposely positioned to prevent the proclivities of corruption and the creation of an aristocracy. The co-mingling of these two branches in a bi-cameral legislature defeats the very purpose of the design of separate and dissimilar bodies as conceived. This has produced the exact state of affairs this system was instituted to prevent.

Time and again during that hot summer in 1787, when the specifics of this branch of government were being discussed, the framers reiterated the need to keep the house of the people anchored to their constituency. Notes taken by James Madison during the Constitutional Conventions held in Philadelphia between May and September of 1787 reveal the clear and undeniable intent of the framers of our Constitution.

During a discussion regarding the origination of spending bills, Eldridge Gerry the delegate from Massachusetts was quoted as saying *"The other branch* (The House of Representatives) *was more immediately the representations of the people. And it was a maxim that the people ought to hold the purse strings"*

John Dickenson from Delaware concurred and, as noted by Madison, the House, as designed, *restrains money bills to the immediate representation of the people"*

George Mason, the delegate from Virginia was more pointed and was quoted as saying that unlike the Senate, the members of the House should be *"chosen frequently and obligated to return frequently among the people"*.

And Alexander Hamilton, *"held essential that the popular branch of it* (a bi-cameral legislature) *should be on a broad foundation"*.

Article One of the Constitution clearly defines the minimum qualifications for a member of the House of Representatives, but Madison was more eloquently specific when he wrote in Federalist #52;

> *Under these reasonable limitations* (requiring that a candidate must be at least 25 years old and a citizen of the United States for no less than 7 years and a resident in the State he is to represent) *the door of this part of the Federal Government, is open to merit of every description, whether native or adoptive, whether young or old, and without regard to poverty or wealth, or to any particular profession or religious faith....As it is essential to liberty that the government in general, should have a common interest with the people; so it is particularly essential that the branch of it under consideration* (The House of Representatives) *should have an immediate dependence on, & an intimate sympathy with the people. Frequent elections are unquestionably the only policy by which this dependence and sympathy can be effectually secured.*

In its current form, Congress has insulated itself from the will of the people by feeding into the factious passions that fund the perpetuation of its existence. Term limits have long been discussed as a solution to this problem, but that measure will only slow the process slightly as succeeding members will be groomed and staged by those who control party funding, office space, committee assignments and therefore, their destinies.

It is a fact that only a well funded candidate can overtake an incumbent or capture a vacant seat. These seats are not for sale outside the established party structure and are rarely seized by a true grass-roots candidate. The funding required to win a Congressional seat obligates the candidate to a predetermined cause and clouds the vision of visionaries who would otherwise hope to break the chain of deceit, creating the Catch 22 that all closed and fraudulent entities establish to maintain order and permanency.

Can we turn a blind eye to the obvious conflict that exists when money so dominates political decision making and that policy flows from the desires of powerful lobbyist's intent on shaping government in their favor? This abomination so fundamentally flaws the system that true and lasting reform can never take hold without a wholesale replacement of members of Congress, the only means that will effectively break this strangle-hold on power.

The House of Representatives has grown to such proportions in both physical size and scope of authority that its very structure is impervious to significant change. From its first quorum in 1789, the House has grown to over 10,000, counting House Members, staff and officers. It has grown so large that in 1995, Congress created its own Chief Administrative Office[7] to provide operations and support services for House Members, at the cost of $120 million annually with its own staff of 730.

This increase in size is the natural out-growth of an ever increasing population, as the system was designed. What must be brought into question is the scope and authority of this legislative body as they serve as

---

[7] CAO Semi-Annual Report July – December 2008 Chief Administrative Office

the self-appointed arbiters over the affairs that determine its own agenda.

Given the enormous breadth and width of influence that this body lends itself to establish jurisdiction over—the extended reach dilutes its ability to adequately focus on salient issues and allows for the wandering attention that provides cover to the representatives, allowing them to avoid the important issues of the day while giving the impression that they are actually executing the people's business. With its 20 standing committees, 3 special committees and 104 subcommittees, there is virtually no part of American life that is untouched by this omnipotent organization. The inability to maintain focus is created by its vast overreach well beyond its Constitutional mandate and gives rise to an oblivious behemoth, unconcerned and unaware of its own inadequacies.

When the 111th Congress took office in January of 2009, the nation was in crisis with national and world economies in free-fall, domestic unemployment nearing 10%, the banking, housing, auto and nearly every other industry in decline—one might think there would be some sense of urgency in their immediate agenda. Not quite… following in a long held tradition of wallowing in self-importance, this latest Congress spent its first days discussing rule changes that favor the new majority, voting to recognize the importance of the 40th Anniversary of National Eye Day and designating Read Across America Day.

Admittedly, it's easy to cherry-pick through the legislative agenda and pull out the most inconsequential issues that the House addresses on any given session. But it is the very essence of this proposed action (the removal of all incumbents from this office in one election) and extremely relevant to point out the colossal waste of time spent on collateral issues that should be outside the purview of a Congress in the first place, let alone one that is dangling on the precipice of catastrophe. Can anyone reasonable argue that in 2009, in America, things are under control and that a collapsed economy, soaring federal deficits and near record unemployment does not represent an impending disaster?

As this new Congress came into session in January of 2009, instead of attending to the critical business of the people, they commence with the following roll-call votes for their first week in office;

- The Presidential Records Act Amendment of 2009. The House votes to "establish procedures for the consideration of claims of constitutionally based privilege against disclosure of Presidential records". A partisan maneuver of spite in an effort to besmirch an out-going President (a pressing matter indeed).
- Presidential Library Donation Reform Act of 2009. The House again votes along party lines, to require all donations over $200 to any Presidential library fundraising organization must now be reported quarterly. (Another spite-full act? You be the judge.)
- The House votes, strictly along party lines, to adopt a resolution to "support the goals and ideas of National Mentoring Month 2009". (A worthy cause to be sure, but is this the priority business of a people suffering the stresses of uncertain futures?)
- On day 4 of this new Congress, they vote to "recognize the efforts of those who serve their communities on Martin Luther King Day and promoting the holiday as a day of national service. (Ditto the note above.)
- The House voted to amend the Rules of the House to "require each standing committee to hold periodic hearings on the topic of waste, fraud, abuse, or mismanagement of Government programs". (Finally a worthwhile effort and an obvious de facto admission of their own incompetence and corruptibility.)

That's only the first week. The first month included such acts of importance as; designating the first week of February National School Counseling Week, honoring the College Bowl Champion Series champion, expressing support for National Data Privacy Day, raising awareness and encouraging prevention of stalking by establishing National Stalking Awareness Month and "supporting the goals and ideals of National Teen Dating Violence Awareness and Prevention Week".

At a most critical time in our nations history, when leadership of the people is not simply necessary but of grave importance, your Representative is spending his time exacting revenge, pandering to irrelevant causes and spending money that must be borrowed while the nation is in crisis and burning down around them. This is not the work of learned men and women performing on behalf of its people, this is the work of narcissistic elites oblivious to the world around them protected within their cocoon of financial support, adhering to their obligatory party mandates.

The predictable argument against this action will come from these pompous delinquents who will tell you the work of Congress is too important to leave to neophytes and the uninformed. They will tell you that their work has deep and lasting consequences that can only be attended to by those connected to the system and well-versed in the ways of an operational bureaucracy. The common man cannot fully comprehend the challenges and complexities of government without their guidance and vigilance on issues affecting our daily lives.

These condescending arguments openly display the complete misunderstanding of the intended nature of the very office they hold and embarrassingly demonstrate their inferiority. They must argue with such great Americans as Alexander Hamilton, James Madison, John Jay and Thomas Jefferson. These men of character and conviction would see these people for who they really are—the self-serving violators of Constitutional intent and contemptible scoundrels betraying their own country for personal gain.

While it is easy to blame the breakdown of the system on the weakness inherent in man given the allure of power—ultimately it is the inaction of the majority that has allowed this system to malfunction so completely. So it would follow, that only an active majority can re-establish the balance needed to repair the system. The scales of justice are tilting from the improper distribution of power and only the counter balance of a re-engaged electorate can replace the void created by complacency.

Chapter Five

Bailing Out

Before I endeavor to discuss the unimaginable amounts of money being spent by the United States Congress (remember, only Congress has the constitutional authority to appropriate money from the U.S. Treasury) it is important that we gain some sense of what a trillion dollars truly is. Simply put, if you were to stack $100 bills 6 feet high, you would need 2.2 football fields to accommodate $1 trillion. Stacks of $100 bills, end zone to end zone, side line to side line, tightly packed to cover every square inch of grass. Now imagine that in fiscal year 2009, Congress has committed itself to spend the equivalent of 6 regulation football fields full of $100 bills stacked 6 feet high. And that's only one year.

Giving you some sense of scale as to the ridiculous amounts of money to be had via the Federal Government, will help you to understand how much of a high stakes game this actually is. While spending on social programs represents the single largest allocation of these funds, so much of this money is up for grabs that it is nearly impossible to separate truth from fiction, good guys from bad guys and the corrupt Washington elite from those with honorable intentions.

Just as the Great Depression gave rise to the Social Security welfare program in 1935, the economic recession of 2007/2008 opened the door to an irresponsible expansion of government spending under the cover of economic recovery and allowed well connected political concerns to further pilfer our treasury, with the help of their willing accomplices' in Congress. Let's examine the recent actions of the 110th and 111th Congress with respect to the spending of your tax and wage withholdings through the self serving declaration of a national crisis.

As the recession that started sometime in 2007 began to affect most Americans, Congress was compelled to take action to help ease the financial strain on their constituents—not so much for the positive effect it may have on the lives of these people, but mainly because in 2008 they would be coming to the voters and asking for their support to return them to office. If a full-blown recession took hold through 2008, their chances of re-election could be adversely affected.

And so, in February of 2008, The Economic Stimulus Act of 2008 was passed. Promoted as a tax relief program with emergency powers, this act granted an instant $600 tax rebate to individuals and $1,200 to married couples, loosely based on incomes, with a minimum of $300 going to taxpayers with incomes under $3,000.

It is no mistake that these tax rebates were timed to reach the Representative's constituency around the same time these same Representatives would be in the district asking for support in the upcoming general elections in November of 2008. This thinly veiled attempt to purchase votes by tossing crumbs to the electorate is no different from the much larger sums that are received by the candidates from their financial supporters for the similar favor of voting on their behalf and retaining their access to federal money. It's evident that this concept of how the world operates is an attitude that occurs in the subconscious of these men and women as this is the standard mechanism of advancement for your Representative and is clearly their default modus operandi.

The wool that was pulled over our eyes came in Title II of this act which increased the loan limits for federally insured mortgages that allowed the Federal National Mortgage Association (Fannie Mae) and the Federal Home Loan Mortgage Corporation (Freddie Mac) to increase their maximum loan obligations – obligations that are insured by the Federal Government (you and me). By increasing these federally guaranteed loan limits, Congress accelerated the sub-prime mortgage market collapse that would soon after launch the nation into a deep economic recession. As further evidence of their deceptive nature, Congress granted the Secretary of Housing and Urban Development (HUD) sole discretionary authority to set these loan limits, thereby abdicating their Constitutional oversight and providing themselves an alibi in case things didn't turn out as planned.

The Congressional Budget Office estimated that the cost to taxpayers for these actions to be in the neighborhood of $168 billion. A paltry sum compared to the madness that was yet to come.

The Emergency Economic Stabilization Act of 2008, enacted on October 3 in the second session of the 110th Congress was a bill to *"provide authority for the Federal Government to purchase and insure certain types of troubled assets for the purposes of providing stability to and preventing disruption in the economy and financial system and protecting taxpayers, to amend the Internal Revenue Code of 1986 to provide incentives for energy production and conservation, to extend certain expiring provisions, to provide income tax relief, and for other purposes"*. Also known as the Troubled Asset Relief Program or TARP, the U.S. Treasury would be allowed to purchase, hold, sell or insure unspecified financial instruments, *"particularly those that are based on or related to residential or commercial mortgages"* according to the Congressional Budget Office. The CBO cost estimate for this program, in round numbers was $700 billion at the time of its passage.

Aside from the complete abandonment of their Constitutional duties with regard to appropriating money from the Treasury, the vague wording and ambiguous instructions for the spending of this money left the bank vault door wide open to waste, fraud and abuse. As if they were too busy to be bothered with properly executing the duties of their office, Congress steps aside and allows industry executives to determine how this money is to be spent to "rescue" the credit markets and their very own banking industry. The purposely vague wording of a bill that allows the federal government to purchase and insure *"certain types"* of troubled assets for the purposes of providing stability and preventing disruption in the economy—or for *"other purposes"* can only be seen as a deceptive measure that, in effect, awards incompetence. There could be no more indistinct or imprecise language used in a legislative bill that spends nearly a trillion dollars of tax payer money.

This Congress was delusional in thinking that they had any understanding as to how to stabilize an economy or prevent economic calamity—as evidenced by the incoherent language of this bill. They were simply mimicking the language of their puppeteers by telling constituencies of the eminent danger of the collapsing credit market without first possessing the facts necessary to make that judgment. (Where I come from, they call that lying.) Instead of the normal procedure used when dispersing such large sums of tax payer dollars; holding committee hearings, enlisting expert testimony on the subject and establishing a learned approach to the problem—their knee jerk reaction was to simply throw other peoples money at an extremely complex set of problems and allow the wolves of industry to secure the hen house of our economy. It could be argued that they were simply duped by the banking and Wall Street lobbyists who exaggerated the urgent nature of failing credit markets in an effort to access federal funds immediately and without the requisite scrutiny such allocation of funds would normally require. I tend to believe the latter since it worked so well for the banking and Wall Street executives who received billions of untraceable federal dollars as a result of this legislation. Either way, Congress' careless and irresponsible decision to approve such an imprecise appropriation of enormous amounts of taxpayer money, represents the highest level of incompetence imaginable.

According to the report from the Office of the Special Inspector General for the Troubled Asset Relief Program, Neil Barofsky, dated April 21, 2009, these funds have been spent, as directed by the office of the Secretary of the Treasury (through the abdicated authority of Congress) on a plethora of industries, entities, politically connected individuals and concerns.

According to this report; 532 banks received $218 billion under the Capital Purchase Program (CPP), $25 billion went to General Motors and Chrysler through the Auto Industry Financial Program (AIFP). (Actually this money went directly to the United Auto Workers Union to adequately fund their under-funded retirement program, a program that fundamentally leads to the collapse of these two auto manufacturers.) $5 billion to the Auto Support Suppliers Program (ASSP), (more union jobs), $15 billion to secure Small Business Administration loans, $70 billion to AIG (a well connected and significant contributor to many members of Congress) as they were classified a Systemically Significant Failing Institution (SSFI) as determined by the Secretary of the Treasury, $419 billion to Citibank and Bank of America through the Target Investment Program (TIP), (more fat cats bailed out by you and me), $75 billion to the Making Home Affordable Program (MHAP) and another $109 billion to *"New programs, or funds remaining for existing programs"* (whatever that means, it's only $109 billion).

But the single largest appropriation of these monies, $1 trillion, went to the Term Asset-Backed Securities Loan Facility or TALF that allowed the Federal Reserve Bank to print money (out of thin air) to provide support for various credit markets.

There is nothing wrong with your math—this Congressional mandate has, as Inspector General Barofsky put it, *"evolved into a program of unprecedented scope, size and complexity"* that will take the original cost estimate from the Congressional Budget Office of $700 billion to nearly $3 trillion over the life of these programs, according to Mr. Barofsky's report.

This inconceivable thievery of the U.S. Treasury in the name of rescuing failing credit markets has done nothing to provide relief to the millions of Americans who have lost their homes and jobs. In fact, the exact opposite has occurred. Since October of 2008, when this bill was enacted, over 4 million Americans have lost their jobs (through May of 2009), according to the United States Department of Labor, Bureau of Labor Statistics. And our nation's gross domestic product (GDP) has dropped at an annual rate of 6.1% (an astonishing rate) in the first quarter of 2009, according to the U.S. Department of Commerce.

And if all that weren't enough to prove the absolute uselessness of these haphazard actions of Congress, Inspector General Barofsky reports that his office has launched 20 separate criminal investigations of fraud, tax evasion and insider trading with regard to the spending of these monies and further represented that these investigations are only the tip of the iceberg of criminal activity in the implementation of this ever expanding federal program.

How can anyone possibly condone or defend the continuing failure and ineptitude displayed by members of this Congress? This act alone will obligate future generations of Americans with additional debt beyond our ability to comprehend.

At this point, it's difficult to carry on. The first two actions noted above represent a level of incompetence and greed that is nearly inconceivable—it's hard believe that it can get worse. Underestimating the assumption of ignorance that Congress has for the people they have been assigned to represent is naive in the extreme. As if their actions take place in the vacuum of the Washington D.C. beltway, they continue to boldly commit acts of larceny on the American people in broad daylight.

In an unthinkable act and unbelievable betrayal of public trust, the 111th Congress, no less than 90 days after the previous Congress passed the Emergency Economic Stabilization Act of 2008, enacts an even larger "Public Law" known as the American Recovery and Reinvestment Act of 2009. With a price tag of $787 billion, this Congress goes on a shameless spending spree, unprecedented in U.S. history. The act, also known as the Stimulus Plan, provided billions upon billions of dollars to every imaginable pet program and personal concern of nearly every member of Congress—a slopping of the bureaucratic pigs of biblical proportions. No special interest, government bottom feeder, campaign contributor or federal office was left out of this buffet, served up to reward compliance and curry favor.

On top of the previously approved deficit spending for fiscal year 2009, this Congress increased funding to almost every category of government; $176 million for "building and facilities" for the Agriculture Research Services, $50 million for Farm Service Agency salaries and expenses, $290 million for Watershed and Flood Prevention Operations, $165 million for the improvement of fish hatcheries and habitat restoration, $11 billion for Rural Housing Insurance Fund Program Account, $1.3 billion for the Rural Water and Waste Disposal Program, $2.5 billion for the Distance Learning, Telemedicine and Broadband Program, $2 billion for Neighborhood Stabilization, $1.5 billion for the Homeless Prevention Fund, $150 million for Economic Development Assistance Programs, the list goes on and on. This smorgasbord of spending sends additional money to the Department of Defense, Department of the Interior, Department of Energy, Department of Agriculture, Department of Homeland Security, Departments of Labor Health and Human Service, Health Information Technology, Transportation, Housing and Urban Development, NASA and the Legislative Branch itself, to name but a few.

This one act of Congress is a mind-blowing expansion of government that will eventually cost the United States taxpayer another $3.25 trillion, according to the Congressional Budget Office, in testimony to a Joint Committee on Taxation.

And just as I have run out of superlatives to describe the brazen disregard for common decency displayed by these barefaced liars in this new 111th Congress, a further abandonment of their sworn duty and due diligence must be noted.

This massive document, the 1,079 page final version of the American Recovery and Reinvestment Act of 2009, was made public and available to the members of the House of Representatives on February 13th—the very same day the Representatives passed it into law, making it physically impossible for any member of Congress to have read it completely. Without reading the text of the act, members of this Congress could not have known exactly how this colossal sum of money was to be spent, they only knew that everyone was getting greased, and that was good for them. In this single act, Congress demonstrated, in undeniable fashion, a clear dereliction of duty, an appalling act of deception and a repulsive violation of the public trust.

The combined effects of these Congressional forays into economic stimulation have netted zero positive affect on the nation's economy. By no measure has the country benefited from these costly acts of desperation perpetrated upon our nation by bungling fools who have so visibly displayed their lack of understanding and competence.

With such devastatingly large amounts of taxpayer money being so frivolously thrown around by those who control our nation's purse strings, it is nearly impossible to accurately comprehend the enormity of the problem created. The multi-trillion dollar debts that have been hoisted upon our nation through these Congressional decries have so adversely impacted the economy that recovery is further away than before any of this insanity began.

These obligations cannot be met by those who have made such financial commitments on our behalf. The amounts are so large that literally, generations of Americans who are not yet born, will be held responsible for these debts. This deprivation cannot go unchecked. What will you say to your children and grandchildren when they realize this burden of debt was allowed to accumulate during your watch? This is nothing short of generational larceny and future tribunals will try those who perpetrated these crimes once the enormity of the problem is revealed in the years to come.

Chapter Six

Crime of the Century

Following and understanding the work of any Congress in the last 50 years is a study in the weakness of man. Granted stewardship over a treasury with seemingly unlimited funds, those who have held this elected position have shown themselves to be incapable of displaying restraint or any sense of self-discipline. The power to direct trillions of dollars awards the men and women of the U.S. House and Senate rock-star status – and just as you might see thousands of screaming fans surrounding a rock-star seeking an autograph, so too are these gift bearing icons surrounded by thousands of adoring lobbyists seeking the same signature that will deliver them a piece of that massive annual budget. Congress is no less susceptible to the pitfalls associated with the delusions of grandeur inherent in idol worship and are too often diminished by these delusions in their ability to demonstrate impartiality and apply common sense.

The systemic failure of this body as a whole taints the entire 535 member institution with the stench of ineptitude as evidenced by a track record of overindulgence and failed policies that has bankrupt a nation.

A simple review of the legislative calendar in any given session of Congress, on any day, reveals an endless parade of political minutia, observable pandering and an incoherent collection of intrusions on the personal life and liberties of the American citizen. With every landing of the gavel, this branch of government imposes mandates and expands a purview that only serves to imperil its people with acts of cold indifference. The recent actions of Congress, noted in previous chapters, do not rise to the level of criminal or treasonous acts only because a docile electorate has granted the perpetrators immunity in the form of reelection. If a criminal act occurs in the private sector, the state is charged with bringing the offender to justice and held accountable for their actions. If a government entity perpetrates a similar act, one that would rise to the level of criminal in the private sector, the voting age population is charged with the duty to prosecute said criminal acts on Election Day. It is *only* because these elected officials are not called out on their blatant flouting of the law by an enraged electorate that these acts are not seen as criminal. But that does not change the fact that they are, or would be, in the private sector. Since a majority of the electorate is not yet enraged, these immoral acts of deception continue to go unpunished.

I am not prepared to place blame on one political party over another for the atrocious conduct of this legislative body as a whole—this will only serve to deflect attention from the issue at hand and condone the endless circle of finger-pointing. Congress has only changed majority party rule twice in the last 50 years and each time, the new majority party in charge has continued the tradition of perpetrating, what I believe to be, the crime of the century. In this despicable act of betrayal and duplicity, we cannot grant tolerance to either party since both have had ample opportunity to correct years of inexcusable conduct and both have continued to profit from the inaction. I speak of course ... of Social Security.

The Social Security Act of 1935 was an act of Congress to provide for a people suffering from the effects of the Great Depression—instead it instituted the largest social welfare program ever attempted by mankind. The 73rd Congress passed a law that was to provide for the general welfare of a specific group of people through a program that Congress would administer, via State government, to provide "*adequate provisions for aged persons, blind persons, dependent and cripple children, maternal and child welfare, public health and the administration of their unemployment compensation laws*".

In this act, Congress expanded its authority to impose a payroll tax to be collected by the employer directly from the pay-check of the employee (what would later become known as the Federal Insurance Contribution Act or FICA Tax). The original amount of the tax in 1936 was 1% for the employee to be matched by 1% from the employer for the purposes of funding this first of its kind, national welfare program. Originally exempted from paying this payroll tax were; farm labor, maids and servants, casual labor, sailors, government employees and charitable organizations. An interesting list of exemptees when you consider that these people represent the labor force of the richest and most powerful entities of the time whose influence on legislation is clearly seen through the blatantly obvious nod to their special interest needs. Congress itself displays an early propensity to place themselves above the laws they make for others by exempting all government employees from this tax as well. This necessary pandering to the Washington elite allowed for passage of a massive bill that granted government an immoral incursion into the paycheck of a non-connected public, living and working outside the benefits of Congressional influence. After years of court challenges to the law and constant public pressure, most of these categories of employment lost their exemption by 1954.

The Social Security Act itself, it can be debated, has no supporting Constitutional authority since nowhere in the Constitution exists a provision allowing government to seize wages from one class of people and pass those wages onto another. The imposition of such a colossal government program and redistribution of personal wealth can only occur in a time of national crisis. The Great Depression of the1930's and 40's provided the necessary distraction that allowed the 73rd Congress to act with such callous disregard of Constitutional intent.

In Title II of this act of Congress, an Old Age and Survivors Insurance Trust Fund (OASI) was established as a separate fund of the U.S. Treasury to collect these taxes, disperse the benefits and accrue interest on the surplus for the purpose of funding the retirement of all those who contributed to the special fund with their payroll taxes. The law required Congress to appropriate funds to the Treasury to deposit into this retirement account in "*an amount sufficient as an annual premium to provide for payments required under this title*". These funds were schedule to grow at a rate of 3%, compounded annually. While this epic act of government was greatly debated and frequently challenged in the courts after its enactment, the trust fund showed early success and by 1948 the OASI Trust Fund had accumulated $10 billion[8] in value as an asset of the American people.

The original Social Security Act has gone through many changes over the years including the creation of a second, separate fund of the U.S. Treasury called the Disability Insurance Trust Fund (DI) as a result of the Social Security Act Amendment of 1956 that expanded the list of beneficiaries. In 1965, Congress enacted another enormous expansion of the Federal Government's authority through the Social Security Act of 1965 that created Medicare and Medicaid as a national health care program to provide care for the aged and poor—all part of a Congressional plan to create a "Great Society". Various other changes in the program occurred over the years including in 1977 when Congress increased the payroll tax rates to 6.15% for both the employee and employer once the predictable failure of this short-sighted attempt at social engineering became an unavoidable fact. Today the rate stands at 7.5% for a total payroll tax to be paid of 15% against all wage earners' earnings.

While this economically destructive act in itself will continue to increase taxes and expand the federal governments influence and control over this nation's population in perpetuity, it does not rise to the level of criminality.

But all of that changed in 1983 when the 98th Congress passed

---

[8] OASI Trust Fund 1937 – 2008, Actuarial Publications, Trust Fund Data Social Security Administration www.ssa.gov/OACT/STATS/table a1

HR1900—signed into law on April 20, 1983. Sold as an action to *"ensure the solvency of the Social Security Trust Funds"* when it became Public Law No: 98-21, this bill, among many other things, added all federal employees including, the President, Vice President, Judges and members of Congress to the Social Security tax and benefits program. It slowed the increase in cost of living adjustments (COLA's) on benefits, raised payroll tax rates yet again and further expanded benefits to numerous other classes of citizens. Buried in the bill, as an amendment to Title VIII of the Administration of the Social Security Act, was a provision that allowed Congress to take the receipts and disbursements of the special (OASI and DI) Trust Funds "off-budget". The language of the bill stated that these receipts and disbursements *"shall not be included in the totals of the federal budget or of the congressional budget and shall be exempt from general statutory budget limitations imposed on federal expenditures and net lending"*.

This language gave Congress the ability to take the surplus cash generated by these changes in law and use it to skew the actual size of our nation's annual deficits and overall debt. It allowed Congress to pay off early investors with current investor's money and spend the surplus (what must be considered profits) on whatever they pleased. The later investors, thinking that their money is being invested to provide the promised returns in retirement, will find that the money never made it to the bank, only a slip of paper representing their money went to the bank. This action, in itself, constitutes the crime for which I speak as it is no different from the crimes perpetrated by the infamous Charles Ponzi who was jailed and deported for the exact same acts of fraud and deception.

Congress's idea of *"ensuring the solvency of the Social Security Trust Funds"* was to increase taxes to generate the annual surpluses the Trust Funds needed to accumulate interest to pay future retirees. After seven consecutive years of Trust Fund deficits (1975 through 1981) Congress needed to change the rules (by raising taxes and reducing benefit increases) to assure growth for the fund. They knew this action would generate large cash surpluses in the program—cash they could use to deceive the public regarding the actual size of the national debt and spend to placate their legions of adoring fans.

Here's how this scam worked. In 1984, the first year after the change to the Social Security Act, the U.S. Treasury collected $6.2 billion more in taxes than it paid out in benefits for the Old Age and Disability Trust Funds. With the changes Congress made in the administration of the OASI and DI trust funds, they were able to take the $6.2 billion in real cash money "off budget" and in return, give the U.S. Treasury a promissory note that they then placed in the Social Security trust funds to replace the cash taken. The Treasury continued to calculate the growth of the surplus funds as if it were real money, as required by law, thereby paying interest on an IOU. Congress then took the cash and placed it in the general fund to give the appearance that the deficit for that year was less than it actually was.

Each and every year after 1983, the Social Security OASI and DI Trust Funds generated ever increasing surpluses (once again, because of congressionally imposed tax increases and benefit reductions). In 1985 the surplus was $11 billion, by 2000 the surplus cash amounted to $153 billion and in 2008, the annual cash surplus to these trust funds was $180 billion. Every year since 1984, Congress has taken this surplus cash from these trust funds and spent the money on things other than what that money was intended to fund. Between 1984 and 2008, Congress has taken a total of $2.4 *trillion* in cash from the Social Security trust fund accounts and given the U.S. Treasury an IOU to deposit. These IOU's or "intergovernmental holdings" as they are known to the Treasury, are held at the Bureau of Public Debt in Parkersburg, West Virginia, in a single, non-descript file cabinet. Worthless pieces of paper that represent the government imposed retirement savings accounts of millions of

American taxpayers.

According to the Bureau of Public Debt, these IOU's and the interest they have earned (if that is even possible) total $4.345 trillion as of June 2009. The actual public debt reported by the Congressional Budget Office in June of 2009 is $7.18 trillion. The real national debt is the combined total of these two amounts. Congress has used a bogus accounting maneuver to misrepresent the indebtedness of the American taxpayer by nearly half. The actual debt of our once prosperous nation currently stands at $11.5 trillion, as of July 1st 2009.

More than 25 football fields, filled with $100 bills sideline to sideline, end zone to end zone, stacked 6 feet high, representing the un-retired debt of the American people. Debt placed on current and future generations of Americans by men and women acting above the fray, protected by golden retirement plans that will ensure their prosperity till death – debt that has crippled a nation and will bankrupt a generation.

The level of corruption and treachery perpetrated by Congress over the last 75 years, regardless of party majority, has risen to a level of criminality never imagined and has condemned our nation to decades of poverty. No argument can be made to defend these actions and no amount of spin can excuse the incompetence. Given the facts regarding these countless acts of unethical behavior and criminal conduct, for any citizen of this country to allow any member of Congress, be it in the United States House of Representatives or the U.S. Senate to remain in office, is an extreme act of treason and cowardice.

To look at the facts, as have been laid before you and somehow extrapolate a reason for returning any of these devious and immoral individuals to office is beyond absurd. Ignorance is no excuse to deprive your children and mine of a future with a chance at prosperity and will label us as the generation that dropped the ball and doomed a nation. The blood of failure will be on our hands if we choose to remain absent in the defense of our Constitutional founding.

The unimaginable prosperity that this country has enjoyed post World War II has simultaneously provided the indulgent life styles we hold so dear and permitted the depravity displayed by our elected officials who have manipulated these prosperous times to allow for their acquisition of permanent and unquestioned power. The people who hold this power and prestige will not willingly relinquish their control of the masses—as is the nature of man. It must be ceased by those who have suffered and will suffer under the yoke of an insurmountable debt and ever depleting liberties. If you have any hope for a better future and real, significant change in the conduct of government, you must first realize that it will not result from actions taken by this crop of individuals. These elected officials will lie, cajole or otherwise deceive the electorate to maintain their strangle hold on power and control of our nations wealth. These patterns in behavior will only change by removing these offenders from office with a unified and overwhelming act of patriotism and national unity that are called for in this message.

This call to action must be on the lips of every American, in every corner of this nation. People who see themselves as a 21st Century American Patriot, taking up arms to defend their current and future opportunities for a prosperous life and the freedoms and liberties guaranteed by our Constitution. There will be no sanctuary for the complacent and compliant citizen who shrinks from this duty to God and country. An uprising is afoot and we must all be prepared to join the fight and spread the word.

The men and women of these United States of America who desire a better life for their children must remove the blinders of bias and political alignment to secure the survival of the America left to us by our parents and grandparents. It is time to rise above the partisanship that divides our strength and unite to form an immovable force of power to revolt against the tyranny of a government out of control and establish a plan to correct these regressions.

Chapter Seven

Silent Majority

I *am convinced that the one thing our* Founding Fathers could not have anticipated is the implausible decline in voter participation. The men and women who stood up to the British crown in order to create a just form of government, laid life and liberty on the line to secure the unalienable, God given rights we now enjoy and, for too many of us, take for granted. I believe it was incomprehensible to these people that after having fought through such difficulties to create these United States, that one day its people would become so complacent with their freedoms and liberties that less than half the persons eligible to vote would actually make the effort to do so.

In a study conducted by Dr. Michael McDonald at George Mason University[9], voter participation in this country is up about 10% since 1996. No doubt as a result of a greater awareness due in part to cable television and its 24 hour news cycle, the World Wide Web and various other advances in technology that has made information more available to the general public. However, the relevant information in this report and reports by the United States Census Bureau is the number of people who do *not* vote.

Off year elections (those that do not involve a candidate for President) beginning in 1998 through 2006, have averaged a 37%[10] voter turnout rate while Presidential elections in 2000, 2004 & 2008 have a slightly greater than 50% voter turnout rate. Over each of these last six

---

[9] Dr. Michael McDonald George Mason University United States Election Project viewed 4/5/2009 http://elections.gmu.edu/turnout_2008g.html

[10] US Census Bureau www.census.gov/population/socdemo/voting/cps2006/tab04a.xls

elections every seat in the United States House of Representatives has been at stake. By averaging out the percentage of voter turn-out rates over the last 12 years, you will find that just slightly over 45% of eligible voters have come out to elect their Congressional representative. With the voting age eligible population averaging around 200 million people over these six elections, approximately 110 million people did not participate in the process to elect their Congressional representative.

These are astounding numbers that defy explanation. The defense of our Constitution is predicated on the participation of the people at large—its creators made that abundantly clear. Having the abandonment of more than half the people in this country of its national duty, it is no surprise that we find ourselves with a national legislature that has no need to provide adequate representation of its citizenry. And why should they?

Unlimited funding provided by special interest concerns has replaced the will of the citizenry by forfeit, allowing members of Congress to attend to the needs of their contributors at the peril of a nation. Having financial superiority over challengers is not a result of good public policy—it is derived from participation in a process that has evolved on Capitol Hill since the beginning. It is naive in the extreme to believe that the millions of dollars in campaign contributions that flow from political action committees (with very specific agendas related to personal profits) do not affect our Congressional representatives voting decisions—they always have and will continue to do so until greater men and women with higher priorities are elected to this office.

This behavior is predictable, given the enormous political power available to these mere mortals. The temptations of corruption begin with an unlimited flow of cash that provides a distinct advantage over challengers, combined with an ignorant public, creates a nefarious amalgamation that allows narrow interests to control the spending priorities of our nation's wealth. When you consider that, on average, each member of Congress controls $5 billion annually in government spending (nearly $14 million a day) you can begin to understand the extent of their power and source of their corruptibility.

The absolute cure for this corruption lies with the 55% of those who have not participated in the process to elect these individuals. The 45% of eligible registered voters who do participate, have historically been split almost evenly along party lines in the last six elections, giving the 110 million people who did not vote a tremendous advantage over these partisans. To imagine that this voting block, in itself, is larger than the combined total of all voters from all political persuasions is difficult to comprehend. The need to tap into this enormous reserve to accomplish the goal of the renovation of Congress is paramount. Given the current political climate and global recession, it should not be hard to motivate just a small percentage of this massive majority to accomplish this task and tip the scales away from predictable partisanship to a more accurate accounting of national sentiment.

If the trend of recent off year elections continues, in 2010 there will be 235 million eligible age voters in America, but only 40% of those people or 94 million, will actually cast a ballot. Six in ten Americans—141 million people will stand idle and allow a minority, evenly split and predisposed to voting along party lines, to return to office the same incompetent representation this country has endured for decades. Career politicians are well aware of the disengaged and are predictably comfortable with the arrangement.

Connecting with the traditional non-voter in off year elections is the challenge this effort faces. Non-voters share a commonality, they choose not to participate. Now that may seem obvious but it demonstrates that there is common ground among those who choose not to participate and provides the link these people have to each other. Typically these people are not partisans but average working Americans with busy schedules and other priorities beyond ignorance. However, they make up the most powerful political force in this country—they lack only the understanding of their significance. Given a simple, specific task to rally around, their power can be realized and influence asserted. The result of their unified actions will renew their faith in this system of government and will command accountability from their newly elected representative.

Getting these people to the polls on Election Day will take a greater effort by the enlightened. The great awakening will only occur after the first successful dissolution of the House of Representatives in one election is achieved. If the potential for historical significance is not enough to get their support, I suggest a reference to their personal finances as a catalyst for their required participation.

For several years I was an instructor at a local community college district, working in the adult education program. Each semester would bring new people into my classroom—working men and women begrudgingly going to night-school after a regular shift, getting the required classroom hours needed to raise their hourly wage. I had an irresistible need to inspire these people and cultivate some sense of national pride. In my many attempts to convince them to take a more active and informed role in local elections, I found one particular discussion that would capture their attention and begin the process of political engagement.

Most of my students earned an apprentice wage, somewhere around $12 to $18 per hour and averaging weekly paychecks around $600. Now, I would first ask them to name their Congressional Representative, State Legislator or City Councilman. Very few knew any of the names of their federal, state or local representatives and even fewer had any understanding of the impact these elected officials had on their lives. I would then ask them how much of the $600 they earned each week did they pay in various taxes and withholdings. Of course that number they knew all too well. Combined withholdings usually averaged around 25%

or $150 per week. Then would come the uncomfortable question/comment—you give someone $600 per month and you don't even know who it is?! Worse yet, you don't even participate in the process to elect the people who decide how much of your money you get to keep each week. A sense of despair would come over the room and the education process would begin.

These working class individuals represent an overwhelming majority of Americans—competent yet distracted. It must be pointed out that whether you choose to participate in the political process or not, the government will remain consistent in collecting taxes and imposing regulation on its citizenry without discrimination. Getting this class of citizens to understand that they hold the key to restructuring government by simply choosing to vote is of the utmost importance to this movement. Tying their inaction to the confiscatory abilities of government is equally important and can be most directly effective through the reference to their weekly paycheck and the associated withholdings. The disenfranchised voter must be made to understand that they can control the amount of taxes they pay each and every week—but only if they get involved in the process.

This is precisely the motivation that must be employed to compel this silent majority to take action—for it is this majority that holds the wealth of the nation. The big dollars that governments need to operate come directly from this class of citizens. There is no money to be had from the overtaxed wealthy—they are too small in number to make a difference when trillions are being sought annually. The real money is with the millions upon millions of wage earners who can be tapped for the few dollars here and there that move to government under the radar and without a fight. Your typical wage earner does not have a tax attorney to create loop holes to legally avoid paying into the Treasury, nor do these people have the financial resources to resist the small but multiple incursions into their wallets by government.

Every time you buy a pizza, a six pack of beer or a gallon of gas, additional fees are tacked on to these purchases that flow from your pocket to government. No transaction takes place without government getting theirs. Decisions regarding these amounts and frequencies are made by people who will ask for your vote in regular intervals. If you do not participate in this process, these public servants will not consider your concerns and will continue to nickel and dime you without fear of retribution.

In California a recent tax increase was placed on every drink served in a bar—a devious tactic to feed my State's insatiable need for more revenues. Every time you drink a beer or order a glass of wine or cocktail in a bar in the Golden State, legislators add 5 cents to the purchase price that goes directly to government coffers. An ingenious plan to add to the State's general fund that goes virtually unnoticed by the consumer. It is only because I stay informed that I know exactly who imposed this burden on this modest pleasure and rest assured, they will feel my wrath come Election Day. There is not a single person that does not work for a government entity who approves of any tax increase but getting these people to voice their displeasure and vote to remove these scoundrels requires that they stay informed and alert. The sad truth is that government does not want you to know these truths and prefers you remain ignorant. How else could such a flagrant overreach be achieved?

The government would rather take $10 from every person who earns less than $50,000 per year than ask for $1,000 from every person who earns more than $200,000 annually. Understanding this standard is critical to inspiring these vast majorities to stay informed and involved. Class envy is the weapon of choice employed by elected officials to distract the majorities from their diabolical plan to get your money, a nickel at a time. Getting even with the wealthy only serves to play on the insecurities of the middle class and creates the diversion necessary to pillage our modest incomes.

Connecting the direct affect your elected officials have on your daily life financially is crucial to motivating the complacent eligible voter. The net result of this unified action will be a greater financial accountability from those who determine how much of my weekly earnings I get to keep and how my tax dollars are spent. This majority, without regard to social or political agendas, understands the simple economic principles that control their life experiences (I can't spend more than I earn) and will demand the same accountability from their newly elected officials.

Minorities with narrow political and financial obligations to special interest concerns will never achieve this standard. This is exactly why there is no reason to fear the new composition of Congress—majorities will always do what is in the best interest of the majority and will be impervious to the dictates of corrupt minorities.

Make no mistake—this is a power grab. Once the majorities awaken to their political power, small minded interests will no longer have the power to dictate policy and spending priorities. The House of Representatives, in the hands of a true national majority will simply set things right. This is the true genius of the creators of the bi-cameral legislature—that the house of the people must be populated by the people, not by politicians. We have for too long accepted that the House of Representatives is a partner of the Senate—it is not! The House was not created for politicians with numerous ties to various political action committees and lobbing groups, begging to feed at the government trough, it was created as the *House of the People*. Only when the people take it back, will the aspirations of our founders be realized.

Returning the House of Representatives to the people will take the participation of traditional voters and non-voters alike. For that 55% of the voting age population who statistically will not participate in the 2010 elections, it is either the sense of impotence that keeps them at home or a complete lack of understanding of the process. Governments have grown so large and seemingly uncontrollable—this perception of impotence is easy to understand. That is why the proposition to dissolve of the House of Representatives in one election is the perfect tool to inspire participation in the process. A direct effect on the future of our country and a chance to make history by employing a clear and simple directive will give the disconnected renewed hope and purpose.

This work can and must be done in the 2010 and 2012 general elections. The incumbent office holder has committed our nation and future generations to debt beyond our ability to comprehend. It is not too late to correct these improprieties and reverse the spending obligations set by those who act with complete disregard for the burdens they have placed on their constituencies. If we do not act to remove these men and women from office, we have no future and will move forward into financial oblivion while remaining a silent majority.

Chapter Eight

Simple Solutions

I *have completely embraced, through my* life experience as an active observer of the human condition, one inescapable truth—life is simple … we complicate it.

Consistently, through historic review and the benefit of hindsight, the solutions to seemingly complex problems have been attainable through the necessity of impartiality and the unavoidable recognition of fact. Our vain attempts at relevancy demand that we interject irrelevant hyperbole consistent with our personal agenda to obscure these facts, less we abandon our position and desired outcome. The simple solutions to life's greatest challenges are often obscured by personal bias and the potential for gain or loss. These complications occur when we choose to serve our own immediate needs by making strained arguments in the face of reality. But one cannot change the obvious—one can only act to provide adjacent distractions in the hope of prolonging or avoiding destiny's inevitability.

One day, perhaps centuries away, when we evolve into beings with a greater understanding of the world around us—through the exponential advances in technology, the toll of time on research and by simple necessity, we will not struggle with the concepts of applied reality. I submit that we are not so far away from that day that we cannot foresee these advances coming. Through an early recognition of these inevitabilities, we can serve to move forward the evolution of our species and provide a better world for those who will follow and prosper as a result of our current actions. In the meantime, we must cast off our naive idealism and face the reality of a lesser man from that that is yet to come.

The current state of man still possesses a Neanderthal need of self importance and personal gain ahead of the concerns for a greater good. Political arguments made in the support of, or opposition to, the challenges of our time are based on these barbaric needs. Rarely do those in a position of political power, with the ability to affect actual change, rise to the occasion and demonstrate leadership in the procession of our evolution. Today's political leaders are only slightly more advanced than their primeval predecessor in that they use the technology available to analyze the vast and real-time polling data that is relied upon to establish their positions on the important issues of the day. Without the overwhelming force of majority opposition, these men and women will continue to conduct their business as usual, reverting to their default position of serving the 15,000 Washington D.C. lobbyists who carry an endless supply of political funding and fawning adulation.

One shinning example of this principle of man's need to complicate life's simplicities can be found in our obsession with diet. Countless diet and weight loss books have been sold to teach, encourage and dictate methods for losing weight and getting the body in shape. Diets of every description and manner continue to top the list of books sold in America, based on topic. Yet the answer to this question is exceedingly simple—eat less, exercise more.

Nothing more can be said in the quest for the truth about diet and weight loss. We can complicate the matter by discussing the differences in genetics or environment and argue that one cannot paint weight loss with such a broad brush, but that will not change the basic fact that, eating less and exercising more is the absolute word on the subject of weight loss. History has proven this to be a sure-fire, can't miss method for getting one's body in shape. We need only take this lesson and faithfully apply the simple solution to solve the problem … done deal.

Certainly there will be those who will object to taking such a simplistic approach to our nation's serious problem of obesity. That dissent will come from someone who is either selling a book, has some other financial gain to be had in the weight loss industry or is working in a government funded research program on the subject. These profiteers serve only to slow the progress toward actual changes in behavior by providing cover for the excuses of those suffering from obesity and its related health risks. They deprive these people of the need to embrace the obvious and to take the personal responsibility of simply eating less and moving more.

I endeavor to make a huge jump in applying this theory of simplicity to a more severe problem that plagues our nation – teen delinquency and gang violence. While there are many contributing factors that place young people in difficult situations, none is more prevalent than the plague of the absentee father. The giant elephant in the room is the tremendous number of fathers that emotionally and physically desert or otherwise abandon their duty as a father. Of course there are absentee mothers who contribute to the problem but their numbers pale in comparison to absentee fathers. And certainly there are abusive fathers who will better serve their child by being absent. These examples are in the extreme minority when discussing the issues related to teen violence and only serve to avoid the obvious.

The men who would shirk from the responsibilities of fatherhood are responsible for so much of what afflicts our country as it relates to crime, helplessness and juvenile delinquency. Because it's not just the children who suffer from this most selfish act, these children grow into adults, ill prepared for life and civil society. Like a disease that grows exponentially, the wake that forms behind these deserters creates a ripple that causes the impoverishment of generations.

Once again, a massive problem that comes with a simple answer. If government can be asked to step outside its Constitutional authority, it should be to demand personal responsibility from its citizenry and there is no greater calling for this application of law than to bring the power of government to bear upon the dead-beat dads that are the scourge of a nation.

This simplistic approach to solving problems finds its greatest opposition in overstuffed bureaucracies. So many have a financial stake in how the trillions of federal funds are spent that road blocks to the obvious and common sense approach to problems are layered like security measures at a death-row prison. These simple answers are locked behind the bars of long-standing institutional obligations to the political concerns of the Congressional enablers.

One such enabler is the Trial Lawyers Association. This single group of Congressional counterparts purchases their unquestioned access to legislators to maintain their control of legislative actions that may harm their industry's ability to profit. So naturally, the simple solutions that involve tort reform get buried under the financial protection of a Congress bought and paid for by this ever-present entity.

Tort Reform is the sacred cow among sacred cows in Congressional parlance. As defined by Wikipedia, *"Tort law is a body of law that addresses, and provides remedies for, civil wrongs not arising out of contractual obligations... tort law defines what constitutes a legal injury and establishes the circumstances under which one person may be held liable for another's injury."*

The problem with tort law, as has been set by precedent in this country, is that it has grown to provide a financial remedy for every injury imaginable, be it real or perceived, physical or mental, assumed or inferred. There are no set parameters to restrict the size or scope of such financial remedies, only that which can be set by a jury. Damage awards for similar injuries greatly vary from state to state and are based primarily on a defendant's ability to pay and there are no limits to what a jury can award an injured party. This creates an unpredictable and open-ended obligation to every individual and business with the slightest assets that may, through the unavoidable interaction with the world around them, become a defendant in a civil action. Protection money that must be paid to insurance companies is stifling for business and creates a huge and unnecessary financial burden for us all. Because insurance companies are usually made to pay these unrestricted awards, the costs for premiums are subjective to the extreme. The simple solution to this seemingly complex issue is clear—limit liability awards so businesses can accurately ascertain their potential exposure and insure accordingly, not excessively.

I am not advocating allowing the negligent to leave the injured insufficiently compensated—I am simply asking for limits to be placed based on a more equitable standard that provides established maximums for awards instead of indefinite perceptions of a defendant's net worth. Congress can act to close this legal avenue to extortion that is allowed under the current convoluted tort system and simultaneously grant the entire country an enormous tax break through the reduced cost for insurance premiums. In one Congressional session, individual and industry alike would be relieved of the undue financial burden placed upon it by a purposely ambiguous application of law. This one simple and common sense change in federal law will provide incalculable economic stimulation immediately and at zero expense to the taxpayer.

No industry will feel the positive effect of this action more so than a struggling health care industry. It is universally accepted that the rise in health care costs for an aging American population will provide the greatest financial challenge to current and future governments. This one change in law will enable health insurance companies to control costs with more certainty and thereby reduce the expense of health care for everyone. The practice of unnecessary defensive medicine will not be completely solved but we will allow the industry to evolve quicker by limiting doctor and hospital exposure to multi-million dollar malpractice awards that are limitless under current law.

A study released through the Civil Justice Report in May of 2006 entitled Medical Malpractice Awards, Insurance, and Negligence: Which Are Related, by Alexander Tabarrok and Amanda Agan, both with the

George Mason University Department of Economics provides irrefutable evidence that capping malpractice awards will effectively and immediately reduce premiums across the board. The report simply states, "*medical malpractice insurance premiums are closely related to medical malpractice tort awards*... and *are related to some factors not rationally related to injuries*". Their research clearly demonstrates the relationship between insurance premiums and medical malpractice awards with statistical evidence that is difficult to argue. The open-ended exposure to unrestricted jury awards creates so much uncertainty for insurance carriers that they must charge higher premiums to the competent doctor to cover their costs for the incompetent. This unreasonably excessive cost of doing business must be passed on to the end-user, needlessly inflating health care costs for all. The report notes that the American Medical Association has made medical liability reform their top legislative priority because according to the AMA "*rapidly increasing medical liability insurance premiums caused by escalating jury awards are seriously threatening patient access to care*".

The report goes to quote the U.S. Department of Health and Human Services who agree that "*the liability crisis is threatening access to care and jeopardizing patient safety*". And in the reports final conclusion the authors refute any claim that premiums are reacting to anything other than awards. "*Our results... support the common sense idea that premiums are driven primarily by awards*".

With a certain health care cost explosion just around the corner, one might think that a Congress, working with the best interest of the people as their top priority, would begin the conversation of tort reform, given the immediate and wide-ranging benefit that such a decisive action would provide to every business and individual in this country.

The unfortunate reality is that trial lawyers and those who reap enormous profits in the personal injury industry, are embedded so deeply in Congress that adherence to their agenda is all but mandatory for survival in office. The enormous political weight that can be brought to bear by this special interest group against any Congressional representative that would initiate such action acts as an unacceptable detriment to doing what is in the best interest of our country.

Ignorance to the obvious that would allow a health care industry to fail and its people to be overburdened by artificially inflated insurance premiums of all types is the bliss these puppets of the tort industry choose to embrace. Your Congressional Representative, as well as mine, has shrank from this fight and will never stand up to this special interest power-house on behalf of a constituency. Instead, they will choose the side of the lawyers and allow them to continue benefiting from glaring gaps in bad law.

This should serve as further evidence that it is certain no significant, structural change in government operations can be achieved without disconnecting the incumbent from the support of his benefactors and re-connecting that representative to the will of the people. The will of the people will provide the majority that will embrace the simple solutions and implement common sense reforms to government on behalf and in favor of the people. This is not idealistic babble, this is a statement of fact that no contorted rebuttal can change. As long as the House of Representatives is home to people who place personal advancement ahead of the greater good of a nation, we will continue adrift in a sea of indebtedness with no hope of salvation.

Chapter Nine

More Simplicity

T*ackling the most difficult issues of* our time does not require complicated plans gleaned from extensive studies—it requires the acceptance of truth and the realization of fact to inspire a common sense approach. It also requires a commitment to change that can only be made real by the application of hard work. Applying this simple logic to effect actual change to the bureaucratic nightmare that is our federal government is a near impossible task given its deep attachment to those who profit amid the confusion. Logic and reasoning are strangers in a world of unfettered access to enormous sums of money and lax accountability. There is little risk in reaping great rewards when you can manipulate the game in your favor and re-write the rules to ensure preferred outcomes.

Clearly, it is the mindset of the current Congress that is not in proper alignment. This management team has no desire to bring about real change—that would just create too many unknowns, one that may include their removal from office. There is no greater concern for your representative than keeping his or her job—accepting this reality is vital to understanding their state of mind and motivations.

This warping is at the center of Congressional psychosis—they do not see the problems from the proper perspective to appreciate the magnitude of a dire situation. From their view, they have all the power, they write all the rules, they can assure their career's longevity and they don't need to appeal to the masses as long as the masses remain unorganized. The problem is not soaring deficits and bloated government—the problem, as framed by the career Representative is how can I do just enough to get reelected without offending the ever present power brokers in Washington D.C.? The common sense approach to problem solving does not exist in this equation.

Without a complete removal and replacement of our nation's management team, we cannot expect our current representatives to even consider the simplest and obvious answers to our most pressing problems. You can expect much of the same—the consistent repeat of past failures. The twisted mind of the career politician thinks the best way to maintain their lofty political and social status is to appease the legions of Washington lobbyists who can assure good press and endless financial support, never considering the possibility that fulfilling the will of the people, by showing political courage to do what they know must be done, as a way of endearing themselves to their constituency to guarantee reelection.

Even after a successful dissolution of Congress is achieved, the difficult work ahead of the new Congress will impact the lives of many who have invested careers in the system and rely on federal funds for sustenance. That segment of our population that feeds on tax receipts for their livelihood, be it a government employee, social welfare recipient, federally funded researcher or government contractor—all will experience this needed change in ways that will inevitably take something away that they have grown accustomed to receiving.

The inescapable fact and our only hope of survival, financially as a nation, involves the reduction in the size and scope of government activity. It is no longer an option to raise taxes to cover or reduce current deficits, because under current law, future spending obligations will demand a rise in tax rates to levels that are absolutely unaffordable and will stifle any hope for growth and prosperity. We are left with only one viable alternative—reduce the size of federal government now.

With very few exceptions, industry and business nationwide has felt the debilitating effects of recessionary times and those who will survive will do so through the necessity of efficiency. An interesting study in survival through the necessity of efficiency can be performed with a look at the rise and fall of General Motors. Interesting because the United States Department of the Treasury is now majority owner of the new GM (NGMCO Inc.) as a result of the tax payer funded government acquisition (the Constitutionality of which is highly dubious) and is the leading force that is reshaping the company post bankruptcy.

The parallel paths of General Motors and the U.S. Federal Government are striking in one obvious aspect—these two entities, representing the two largest employers in the country, created overly generous health and retirement benefits programs for their employees (GM began offering its employees health insurance and pension benefits in 1950, while the U.S. Congress, through the Treasury collects and disperses benefits not only to workers who have paid into the system but also to a large group of people who have not, as a result of the Social Security Act of 1935). These severely flawed programs that over-promised benefits and underestimated the rise in future health care costs ultimately lead to the financial collapse of General Motors and will absolutely bankrupt the U.S. Treasury.

While GM willingly entered into these severely flawed labor agreements, the U.S. Taxpayer, the under-writer of the Social Security promises, had this contract imposed upon them by a board of directors who had no stake in the company bottom line.

Regardless the reasons for entering into such disastrous agreements, NGMCO Inc. now has a simple, common sense plan that will assure their reemergence—a plan devised by a branch of the federal government that applies logic to fact based on historically proven methods for successful recoveries. Congress, acting through the U.S. Treasury, has agreed as part of the GM bankruptcy filing[11], to enact the following plan; reduce labor by 1/3 (U.S. employees), eliminate 35% of management positions, discard inefficient brands (Saturn, Hummer,

[11] "The New General Motors Company Launch Today" GM Press Release 10 July 2009

Saab and Pontiac), close 1/3 of its factories and parts operations and eliminate 50% of its new car dealerships.

Drastic yet necessary steps that will undoubtedly save this company and assure its future viability. History has shown these austere methods to be successful and the U.S. Taxpayer may one day reap the benefits with the possibility of a future return on their $62 billion[12] investment in this new, restructured company. Once again—a big problem with a simple and obvious solution.

Unfortunately this simple solution comes at a great expense to the thousands upon thousands of American's who will lose their jobs as a result of these difficult but necessary actions. According to the U.S. Bureau of Labor Statics, unemployment in the state of Michigan has reached 15.2% (and climbing) as of July 2009, making it the hardest hit area in the United States. Thousands of the new car dealerships across the country designated for shut-down, many which have existed for nearly a century, were summarily closed with the stroke of a pen, ending the careers of these owners and many of their employees. And iconic automotive brands were beheaded by the hardened steel axe of efficiency.

Much pain and sorrow will be the by-product of this necessity for change. As a result of the severe downturn in the American economy, many have suffered similar fates with companies from nearly every industry struggling to restructure for survival. With nearly 6 million jobs lost in this country from December of 2007 through May 2009, very few have gone unscathed during this exceptionally complex economic slump. There are arduous times yet ahead and many more will suffer from the debilitating effects of this unique, yet cyclical recession, until the inevitable recovery begins.

That inevitable recovery can be hastened through the actions of a

[12] "GM Collapses Into Government Arms" Neil King Jr. & Sharon Terlep Wall Street Journal 2 June 209

competent Congress who will apply the same sober measures it has mandated for NGMCO in their effort to avoid bankruptcy for the U.S. Treasury. The rank and file labor, management and offices of the federal government must also face the executioner as reductions in the size and scope of government activity is an irrefutable and absolute requirement for their continued existence.

This is the unavoidable truth of our time—just as every industry in America has had to downsize to remain solvent, so too must the federal government face the obvious need to reduce expenses through reorganization. While we will all share in the hard work and personal sacrifice that awaits us in the years ahead, in no way can Congress exempt itself from these burdens of sacrifice. Congress has demonstrated the ability and recognition of the need to implement sound financial principles for the recovery of the auto company they now own. How can they then deny our country the same application of sanity in correcting the similar financial catastrophe that faces the people they serve?

Do not expect the current body of men and women on Capitol Hill to carryout this mandate, they have shown themselves to be deficient in this regard and have given no indication they would even consider such sacrifice. To the contrary—incredibly, Congress is contemplating yet another massive expansion of government in the summer of 2009 by proposing a new national health care program that will, in effect, nationalize the private sector health care industry. To demonstrate their complete detachment from the reality that surrounds them, they plan to exclude themselves from the mandate they will impose on the entire population of these United States[13]. Their one observable flash of intelligence knows that this plan is disastrously defective and will not suffice for *their* health care needs.

This difficult task can only be carried out by people of character and strength—men and women without obligations to those who will lose

[13] HR3200 111th Congress 14 July 2009

jobs, money and prestige as a result of government restructuring. And just as GM has had to face the reality of job losses, management cuts and the elimination of out-dated brands and operations, so too must government face the truth of this logic. We face a level of sacrifice similar to the greatest generation of World War II. As in the years leading up to WWII, we face a similar uncertainty and direction—but we know deep down what must be done.

I do not wish to overstate the facts or draw improper comparisons but this is the top story of our time as we have come to a clear crossroads on the path to our nation's future. We may one day hope to adequately measure up to the accomplishments of the Greatest Generation if we can focus our fight to preserve the blessings of freedom and liberty. Do we succumb to an oppressive government that will do for us and tell us what to do? Or do we take action to restore our independence, freedom and liberties? Simply because it is not the lead story on the evening news does not diminish its immediate importance. Facts are a stubborn thing and the fact is we face certain catastrophic financial collapse without a change in our battle plans to face our internal enemy.

This enemy will resist every attempt to reduce their ranks and dilute their power and influence. The simple steps that must be taken to correct our national direction will be at the expense of the entrenched politician and civil servant. They must come to know that they are not exempt from the sacrifice most Americans have had to endure through this exceptionally difficult recession.

Antiquated, inefficient and redundant government operations must be eliminated. Social entitlements must be reserved for only the truly needy among us and the able-bodied will be removed from these roles. Overhead and staff must be reduced across the board increasing work-loads for some while other less competent employees will be shown the door.

The federal government employees approximately 2.7 million people according the United States Bureau of Economic Analysis. The average federal employee earns $106,871 annually in wages and benefits compared to $53,288 in the private sector. And while the private sector has been forced to eliminate jobs and reduce wages as a result of this recession, government employment has continued to grow and flourish. A news release by the BEA in June of 2009 showed that while private sector wages and salaries decreased by $12.4 billion nationally in May of 2009, Government wage and salaries increased by $3.9 billion that same month. This imbalance will be the prime target of the cost cutting measures that will be employed as part of the plan to reduce overall government spending.

Priority spending will negatively affect the arts, science and national education programs as these electives will be given back to the states for funding. It is not a pleasant proposition for any American—it is simply a necessity that must become a reality to avert national insolvency.

Every aspect of federal spending must be examined and evaluated for efficiency and need. No entity will be seen as untouchable as the burden must be spread evenly across the vast reaches of government programs and expenditures. Life as we know it will change for the many who will suffer from this much needed reorganization of national priorities. The reduction in entitlements will adversely affect the most vulnerable segment of our society in the short term, but a rejuvenated economy will allow private sector charity to fill the void post recovery.

This is not about exacting revenge on self-indulgent government—this is about saving a nation from financial ruin. This is about doing what must be done to rectify years of reckless spending and unaccountable behavior. We have been placed in this position by selfish overlords who have pillaged our wages and maxed-out out credit for half a century. No one will take pleasure in the difficult work of reorganization and restructuring that will inflict financial pain on nearly every government funded entity. This is not of our choosing but it has become our burden.

A new Congress cannot be held accountable for these shameful acts, but it will be accountable to restore order.

We cannot shirk from this—the calling of our time. It is time to take inventory of all you hold dear and ask yourself what level of sacrifice you are willing to endure to keep what you and your parents have worked so hard to create.

We can be certain that the net result of these harsh actions will be a renewed economy and a return to more prosperous times. The strength and spirit of America will quickly restore order and the amazing machine of our prosperity will rev faster once the weight of government is lifted from our lives.

I am not unaware of the idealistic nature of this vision for our future—I recognize that to accomplish such lofty feats requires a coordinated and far flung effort to bring the believers and non-believers to this fight. But naiveté does not preclude the truth. The strength to acknowledge the facts and accept an obvious course of action, no matter how preposterous or impractical, will require a leap of faith—faith in your fellow American and faith in yourself. This is the land where the impossible is possible as the people of this great country have shown time and again.

Do not be so quick to doubt the power of a freedom loving people to recognize the obvious and apply the simplest of measures to bring about a great change. It is as simple as saying no.

Chapter Ten

What Must You Do For Your Country

When John F. Kennedy spoke the now famous words, "*ask not what your country can do for you – ask what you can do for your country*" he was asking Americans to join together in the historic effort of, "*defending freedom in its hour of maximum danger*". Our newly realized ability to destroy all mankind through the use of nuclear weapons constituted the maximum danger for which he spoke. This was not a specific call to action, but a request for the people of this country to come together and "*join in the struggle against the common enemies of man*". President Kennedy knew that a united United States of America could face down any danger or threat to its freedoms and sovereignty. His call for unity and the strength that unity inspires has always provided the foundation on which this country has been built.

The question—what can you do for your country, as referenced here, addresses a far greater effort than that of supporting the proposal to remove incumbents from office. This question is now asked so that the hard work of problem solving can begin. What can you do for your country? What can you do to assure prosperity for future generations of Americans? What can you do to demand greater accountability from elected officials? What can you do to restore the promise of our founding?

This call to duty cannot be forced upon those unwilling to accept responsibility for their own actions or the actions of their leaders—this call can only be heard by those eager to participate in the defense of our Constitution. It is far too easy to take advantage of the generosity of the state, than to participate in the hard work that provides this generosity.

The need to assume personal responsibility for your actions and the actions of those whom you support is *exactly* what you can do for your country. From demanding accurate representation to giving your employer eight full hours of the work they are paying you for—making this country great is the responsibility of all who bask in its greatness.

Just as you provide for your family, so too must you provide for your country if you hope to continue living the remarkable life to which we have grown so accustomed. To preserve this standard of living we will all be called upon to do what we can for our country. Difficult times are no doubt ahead and the need to pay attention, stay involved and work in concert with those around you to maintain our national household is an absolute necessity. Your country needs you to make informed decisions and demand truth from government. Your country needs you to proficiently produce the goods and services that generate the prosperity we all share. No one who walks streets made safe by police or drive roads that are straight and level is excused from the call of national duty. Your partaking in consuming all that this country has to offer requires your participation in the process that assures this bounty.

Assumptions made that the quality of life we lead is a right guaranteed by government are incorrect and deeply flawed. The quality of life we enjoy is directly related to the effort put forth by the individual, working within the laws and rights protected and enforced by government. There is no guarantee of happiness and prosperity other than that for which we provide ourselves. Government's job is to ensure these rights are protected and evenly applied to all who live and work within the prescribed guidelines of a civil society.

Correcting decades of financial mismanagement will require an extraordinary effort and sacrifice from which no American will be exempt. Reducing spending and limiting the size and scope of government will take something from everyone and everyone must be willing to accept the challenge to persevere and replenish. We absolutely have the capacity to restore prosperity and preserve liberty through the hard work and ingenuity that is the hallmark of this nation. But not without significant structural changes in the way the business of our country is conducted and our nation's wealth spent. The answers are simple—it is the consequences after obvious measures are deployed that will require national sacrifice and is where this argument becomes partisan.

In the private sector, it is simple survival of the fittest—natural evolution in action. There is only one absolute requirement for survival in the private sector and that is bottom line profits. If you can more than fund your operations with your current revenues, you will continue to grow and prosper. Countless fortunes have been built and unimaginable technological advances have been achieved through the mechanism herein known as private sector principles. The healthy, safe and plentiful lives we lead are due primarily to free markets that gave birth to advances in medicine, transportation, science and every imaginable aspect of our existence in the 21st Century.

Televisions, automobiles, trains, planes, plastics, vaccines, artificial organs and computers—you name it and it was created in the private sector by companies whose expenses did not outpace its revenues. The lives of generations of Americans have been enhanced, not only by the products created in the private sector, but through the wages paid to the employees of these companies who prospered as a result of their hard work—a true win-win situation.

The role played by organized labor in establishing livable wages and employee protections cannot be understated in the evolution of the American worker. Today, these principles are applied throughout the nation's work force in both union and non-union environments alike. Work place rules have become universal and the protections enforced by government are required in both public and private sector employment thanks to the efforts of these labor unions.

By their very nature, governments do not have the same obligations to the bottom line or even to provide a level of competence sufficient to provide customer satisfaction—both absolute necessities in the private sector. If government could be required to adhere to a modified version of private sector principles, we can begin to build solid ground on which both sides of this dangerously partisan issue can find as common.

There are obvious areas in government such as the military and space exploration that free market principles cannot be applied, but there are enormous opportunities throughout government where these principles can and must be implemented. In some way, government must be made accountable to the limits of its revenues. By requiring the thousand upon thousands of government agencies, offices and operations to increase their efficiencies, jettison redundancies and become accountable to a reduced budget that will inevitably flow from the overall reduction in government spending, we can begin the work of returning balance to our nations finances. We cannot allow public sector, taxpayer funded operations to continue to operate in the red without the mandate of correction. Government must be required to attend to the same level of bottom line effectiveness and efficiencies that the private sector cannot avoid.

Most, if not all adult Americans have encountered government inefficiencies—it's a national joke and a deteriorating truth that can no longer be laughed off. My personal experiences would make a sad recount of watching tax dollars at work, employing people with no motivation, concern or awareness of the world around them—listlessly walking through the inconvenience of serving the public.

I take no pleasure in pointing the finger of blame at public servants, I blame their lack of motivation on a system that rewards longevity over ability – a system that institutionally provides no standards for excellence and protects incompetent behavior under the guise of tenure. By applying the private sector principle of measurable performance standards, we can weed out the dead wood and promote achievement. In the arena of civil service, this self-examination falls to the labor unions that overwhelmingly and almost exclusively represent these workers.

There was a time when unacceptable working conditions and ruthless management ran rough-shod over unorganized labor. Those days have been eliminated primarily through the formation of the labor unions who established rules that have influenced work place standards for all wage earners.

Unfortunately that pendulum has now swung so far in favor of the worker that a more equitable balance must now be reached. The life threatening work of public safety employees should no doubt be rewarded by lucrative pay and sufficient retirement offerings. For these men and women I have the greatest reverence and apologize for any bundling with less dangerous jobs within your union ranks that may be inferred herein. We are blessed that there are those who would put their lives on the line to protect and serve the public. To these people, every over-the-top benefit is appropriate given the sacrifice made by them and their families. It is the balance of those in public service who must ask themselves if they are providing a level of excellence commensurate with their prevailing wage income.

Major corporations as well as state and city governments across the nation are suffering financial losses under the conditions of collective bargaining agreements made during prosperous times that overpromised life time benefits and unrestricted access to health care. These luxuries cannot be maintained under current financial conditions and the ever rising costs of medical care. Those who are vested in these programs will continue to prosper under standing agreements – it will be those people who, moving forward, will not be so fortunate. In order to prevent national economic failure, the rules must be changed to restrict future labor contracts from including benefits in perpetuity and those who choose public service will be asked to accept a lesser standard that will be primarily driven by performance and revenues.

This will be the calling of future generations—to rely less on government coddling and more on self reliance. Ask not what your country can do for you, because your country is you. The question that should be asked, what can I do to improve myself and the improved conditions of the country will follow. The limit of our federal government's ability to provide services for its people has long since been breached by the ever-increasing entitlements that can no longer be sustained. The government does not create wealth or generate profits—it takes money from the producers and spends that money to fund its many operations and public services. If you are a wage earner in this country, 81% of all the money the government has to spend each year comes directly from taxes levied on your wages. Another 12% comes from corporations that can manage to turn a profit annually. There is no other single entity that significantly contributes to our national coffers.

Requiring the federal government to live within its means can only be achieved by a Congress that can act without fear of retribution from those who feed at a government trough filled with our wages and profits. But what retribution can be had when a Congress is seated that is not enslaved by the takers of our nations wealth or driven by the need for permanency? The actions that must be taken to end the cycle of borrowing beyond our ability to pay can only be accomplished by a Congress that has severed its ties with the Washington insiders and will represent the true will of the people.

It can be no other way—until we act in unison to elect people outside this cabal, our future will be lost to the greed that continues to grow mountains of unserviceable debt.

Chapter Eleven

All That Unites Us

I *refer often to our nation's Founding Fathers* and the Constitution they created as the foundation upon which this action is based. I have a great reverence for the work of these men and the sacrifice made by their families to form the nation that has provided so much prosperity for so many people. The creation of this form of government and the work of those who have kept its promise has moved the evolution of mankind forward at a pace unequaled in historic record. Our nation's founding documents put in place a government that has allowed its people to prosper beyond anything imaginable to its writers. The lifestyle and access to excess that every American enjoys today is a direct result of the difficult suffering and subsequent success of the colonists who founded our first thirteen states. Our connection to these people cannot be lost to history and must be kept alive in the hearts and minds of every inhabitant of this great land.

The resulting success of their work is undeniably significant to all mankind. These United States of America are not only the most powerful force on earth, both financially and militarily, but we are also the most benevolent. Never before has a nation wielded so much power, yet acted with so much compassion. This is the promise of our founding and the moral adhesive that inspires the connection we have to each other as Americans.

Today most Americans live the lifestyle of a King, by 18th Century standards. Simple conveniences like indoor plumbing and access to abundant stores of food are today, so easily taken for granted. The standard of living for the average American is so much greater than any society has ever approached—yet there are those among us who do not recognize the source of their fortunate existence. Not all the people of the great land see the inherent goodness and abundant opportunity that our Constitution provides and protects.

The narrative of our nation's history, for some, is one of oppression and corporate greed. They see the work of our military to maintain world peace and protect our national interests wherever they may exist, as expansionist and imperialistic. There are many whose life experience has drawn them to these conclusions – those who have experienced prejudice, injustice, poverty and hopelessness in the land of plenty. I cannot begin to provide redress to all, but we do not want to exclude them from the work at hand. I can only implore these people to look at the world around them and focus on that which unites us. The force and power of the many will ultimately bring justice and peace to those among us who have the genuine desire to better ourselves and the lives of those around us.

I have been blessed with the gift of historical perspective. I do not feel so far removed from those who came before me and built this nation from coast to coast. It is the work of our predecessors that I see as the reason for the bountiful life we live today. I do not take for granted that the extensive highways, railways, water delivery systems and sewers are here only through the hard work and common goals that only a unified nation can achieve. The fact that I can get in a car that can reach speeds in excess of 100 mph and travel anywhere in this country, with fuel stations and safe lodging all along the way is proof of the greatness we all share. Spend a weekend in Las Vegas and try to tell me Americans have it difficult in the slightest. And while our lifestyles approach decadence, we must remember that we have earned, through hard work and dedication to family and country, every luxury in this life we are afforded.

The achievements of Americans on this continent are a result of the collective work of men and women of all races, creeds and histories.

People from every corner of this planet have come here to share in this prosperity and have worked side by side to create the life we experience today. No one group or concern stands above another in the accomplishments of our people. Together we have shown the world and ourselves that nothing is impossible for a free people, unencumbered in the pursuit of prosperity and happiness.

Unfortunately there are those among us who wish to undermine our access to that happiness and prosperity. They have found success only through the means of dividing us. The deep political divisions that are so evident today are not a result of the breakdown of the American spirit, but through the works of those with narrow personal agendas who categorize and victimize individual groups in an effort to pit American against American for the purpose of personal, political or financial gain. It is only through these means that our collective patriotic spirit can be diminished. We so easily fall prey to the propaganda of spin and allow ourselves to be classified and pigeon holed into groups created to inspire opposition with each other.

Those people on the opposite side of the street at some political rally or protest are the same people who we anonymously high five at a sporting event to celebrate a local team's success. We do not ask for political affiliation before we shake the hand of someone we meet or hold open a door to a stranger as a gesture of courtesy. And no country can unite more seamlessly than the United States after such events as the attacks of 9/11 or the destruction caused by natural disasters. There is so much that unites us it seems ridiculous that there exist such political divisions that only serve to inhibit our ability to reach our potential and grow our prosperity.

The greatest advances of mankind have come from the people of this country, working together to achieve a common goal. Impossible acts like landing a man on the moon and splitting atoms are the work of a free people united behind a single goal of achievement. There exists no test of political compatibility within the scientific community that accomplished these great feats any more than religious or social standards prevented men and women from working together to build the infrastructure that connects our nation.

The success or our country comes from the hard work of the responsible individuals that dominate our ranks. While the fringes of social behavior, both far left and far right are painfully on display through multiple media outlets trying to expand an audience—the overwhelming majority of us is busy putting in our 40 to 60 hours every week, continuing the work of nation building. The constant barrage of left versus right political minutia is only employed to generate ratings and is simply the work of marionette's trying to achieve relevance. We should not be fooled into believing these extremists are representative of our national spirit. The 24 hour news and political commentary shows that flood our radio and television airways with partisan dribble are merely theatre and their attempts to impact social behavior can only succeed through our acquiescence. It is only because we are distracted by the work of raising families and paying mortgages, coaching little league and squeezing in a round of golf do we seem irrelevant to those who make a living discussing political matters from on high. They have greatly underestimated our strength, numbers and commonality.

The potential that we have to render these pundits and political spin doctors impotent is immense. While they are fighting over the scrapes of insignificant minorities, our majority can lap the field with the unified action of reseating the House of Representatives in one election and send these experts home with the gift of irrelevance.

I do not mean to imply that this action alone will change the world—it is just the first step. A complete realignment of political thought will follow in the success of a decisive Congressional shake-down by the people at large. In the past, well focused political action committee's, labor organizations and corporate entities determined the outcome of elections and social policy. These groups will be replaced by a unified, supermajority that will continue to act in unison until the desired results are in place. Because after a complete dissolution of the House of Representatives is achieved, every legislative action going forward will be done in the best interest of the people of this country and not to the benefit of the aristocratic money changers.

We are a great and powerful nation, not because of the leadership of a dictator or under the boot of an oppressive military, but because we are a free people, exercising our God given right of self determination and the pursuit of happiness and prosperity. Our Constitution acknowledges and guarantees these rights and it is only the people of this great nation who can insure these rights will exist intact for future generations of Americans to enjoy and extend.

The preamble to the Constitution unambiguously establishes the intent, desire and expectation of the creators and serves as the base foundation upon which the entire document stands. Its meaning cannot be seen in any shades of gray. It reads *"We the People of the United States, in Order to form a more perfect Union, establish Justice, ensure domestic Tranquility, provide for the Common defense, promote the general Welfare and secure the Blessings of Liberty to ourselves and our Posterity, do ordain and establish this Constitution for the United States of America"*

Undoubtedly we have formed a more perfect union and established justice. Government has fulfilled the obligation to provide for domestic tranquility, the common defense and the general welfare of its people. But the task of securing the Blessings of Liberty to ourselves and our Posterity unmistakably falls to the people. In order to secure the blessing of liberty for ourselves and our children, we must not allow the natural incursions of government to slowly erode that which is constitutionally ours. The fight for liberty occurs every time government attempts to take something more from its people. It is the nature of a ruling class to continually extend its control over it subjects. We must be assertive in the handling of our business of performing our role as the protectors of this remarkable blessing.

This *is* the calling of our time. We are at a clear and decisive crossroads in American history. The choices are obvious—do we continue to allow for an ever expanding Federal government to take control over more and more aspects of our lives through taxation, regulation and imposition of government mandates? Or do we insist that the principles enumerated in our founding documents concerning freedom and liberty be adhered to through fiscally responsible government and accurate representation?

It is time to speak up America. You have a chance to change history by simply exercising your constitutionally protected right to vote. You need only take this one vote on your national ticket to make the clear and unmistakable statement that we the people are taking back our government for ourselves and our children. We will correct our collision course with financial ruin and insure that the America we will leave to our children will be better than the one we were born into.

There is nothing in our political future that would indicate that any change of national direction is imminent—only this action. I have an unbounded confidence in the spirit of Americans to come together behind this movement and bring with them the complacent and disconnected voter to double, triple and further multiply our votes to remove the incumbents from office. This is a simple yet enormously effective effort that will determine the future of our country and establish a new national call to action and duty. The voice of the average American will be heard above all others and the American spirit of our founding will be reborn and embraced to form an immovable force dedicated to the defense of our Constitution and the preservation of our liberties.

I was at first contemplating a witty catch phrase to suit a slick advertising campaign in order to promote this idea. I have concluded that the importance of this action does not lend itself to such frivolities.

The work of reseating our national legislature is a serious and urgent matter that cannot be assigned a strained acronym or insufficient title. We must come together to take back the House of Representatives for the people by voting to remove the incumbent office holder in each and every Congressional district in the country. The immense ripple effect that this coordinated action will create will be felt in every quarter and will inspire a more accurate representative form of government throughout the land. No two or three word summary can capture the significance and importance of this work.

Carry forward this message—your one vote can and will make a difference if properly placed. This government can be reined in and control returned to the people. We can stop this freight train of runaway government and restore confidence through the realignment of our system. There is no other way to change that which seems irreversible except through the unified efforts of a people driven by a patriotic spirit and with the blessing of their Founding Fathers.

Epilogue

Our nation's Founders Fathers purposely made revolution exceedingly simple to achieve. The ability to overthrow a government out-of-control can happen, literally overnight. On the first Tuesday in November, in even numbered years, the citizens of a great land are afforded the opportunity to reinstitute their government with a single vote on a single day.

The following instructions will arm you with the only weaponry you will need to perform your patriotic duty and become part of a national revolution.

When you first receive your ballot, locate the selections for the candidates for the United States House of Representatives. The incumbent will be clearly identified—simply do not vote for this person. Carefully select from the remaining candidates for this seat and select that person whose positions most accurately reflect your attitudes. It will not be of significance that you may vote for someone you do not know – the only thing that is important, is that you ***not*** vote for the person listed as the incumbent.

As stated earlier, if party affiliation is important to you, then feel free to start the revolution months earlier by voting to nominate a candidate from your party in the primary elections—as long as it's not the incumbent. Either way, you will have fulfilled your role as a patriotic revolutionary and changed the world with a simple stroke of the pen, punch of a card or tap on a key pad.

Secondly and equally as important – you must inspire as many people as you can to do the same. Everywhere you go and everyone you meet must know of this singular act of patriotism. This is truly the calling of our time – do not deprive your family or friends the opportunity to be part of a national movement and a chance to make history.

There will be 130 million Americans who will choose not to vote in the upcoming elections – 6 in 10 people you know hold the key to saving our great nation and restoring the promise of our founding. The only motivation needed to reconnect these people to their country can be found herein. Share this message, motivate the complacent and do not rest until this important work is complete.

This cannot be seen as some unnatural imposition on those around you—proudly proclaim the power of this silver bullet and share the glory of saving our nation with your neighbors, co-workers and casual acquaintance. *The 21st Century American Patriot* will inspire the strength to open the eyes of every American to the truths that surround us and provide the key to preserving the blessings of freedom and liberty, bestowed upon us by the undeniable genius of our Constitution.

www.ingramcontent.com/pod-product-compliance
Lightning Source LLC
LaVergne TN
LVHW020650100826
845148LV00012B/2411

9780982186725